Mastering
IT Project Management
Concepts, Techniques, and Applications

Nikhilesh Mishra,
Author

Website
https://www.nikhileshmishra.com

Copyright Information

Dedication

This book is lovingly dedicated to the cherished memory of my father, **Late Krishna Gopal Mishra**, and my mother, **Mrs. Vijay Kanti Mishra.** Their unwavering support, guidance, and love continue to inspire me.

Table of Contents

Author's Preface

Welcome to the captivating world of the knowledge we are about to explore! Within these pages, we invite you to embark on a journey that delves into the frontiers of information and understanding.

Charting the Path to Knowledge

Dive deep into the subjects we are about to explore as we unravel the intricate threads of innovation, creativity, and problem-solving. Whether you're a curious enthusiast, a seasoned professional, or an eager learner, this book serves as your gateway to gaining a deeper understanding.

Your Guiding Light

From the foundational principles of our chosen field to the advanced frontiers of its applications, we've meticulously crafted this book to be your trusted companion. Each chapter is an expedition, guided by expertise and filled with practical insights to empower you on your quest for knowledge.

What Awaits You

- **Illuminate the Origins:** Embark on a journey through the historical evolution of our chosen field, discovering key milestones that have paved the way for breakthroughs.

- **Demystify Complex Concepts:** Grasp the fundamental principles, navigate intricate concepts, and explore practical applications.

- **Mastery of the Craft:** Equip yourself with the skills and knowledge needed to excel in our chosen domain.

Your Journey Begins Here

As we embark on this enlightening journey together, remember that mastery is not just about knowledge but also the wisdom to apply it. Let each chapter be a stepping stone towards unlocking your potential, and let this book be your guide to becoming a true connoisseur of our chosen field.

So, turn the page, delve into the chapters, and immerse yourself in the world of knowledge. Let curiosity be your compass, and let the pursuit of understanding be your guide.

Begin your expedition now. Your quest for mastery awaits!

Sincerely,

Nikhilesh Mishra,

Author

CHAPTER 1

Introduction to IT Project Management

In the rapidly evolving landscape of Information Technology (IT), successful project management has become paramount. Welcome to the world of IT Project Management, a dynamic and critical discipline that ensures the efficient delivery of technology solutions, from software development to infrastructure upgrades. This introductory chapter sets the stage for your journey into the realm of IT project management, shedding light on its definition, significance, and the pivotal role of IT project managers. We'll explore the unique challenges faced in IT project management and unravel the immense value it brings to organizations in achieving their strategic goals. Whether you're a seasoned IT professional or a newcomer to the field, this chapter will lay a solid foundation for understanding the intricacies of IT project management. Let's embark on this exciting journey together.

A. Defining IT Project Management

Information Technology (IT) Project Management is a specialized discipline focused on planning, executing, and overseeing projects within the IT domain. It encompasses a systematic approach to deliver IT projects on time, within budget, and in accordance with predetermined quality standards. At its core, IT project management is about harnessing resources, both human and technological, to achieve specific objectives, whether it involves developing software applications, implementing hardware upgrades, or optimizing IT infrastructure.

The Key Components of IT Project Management:

1. **Project Scope:** Defining the boundaries of the project, including its objectives, deliverables, and limitations, is crucial. A well-defined scope prevents project scope creep, which can lead to delays and budget overruns.

2. **Project Schedule:** Establishing a timeline with milestones and deadlines is essential for tracking progress and ensuring timely completion. Tools like Gantt charts are commonly used to visualize and manage project schedules.

3. **Resource Allocation:** Assigning the right personnel and technology resources to various project tasks is a balancing act. Effective resource management ensures that the project moves forward efficiently.

4. **Budgeting and Cost Estimation:** IT project managers must create realistic budgets and continuously monitor costs to prevent financial overruns.

5. **Quality Assurance:** Ensuring that the final product or solution meets the specified quality standards and fulfills user requirements is vital. Quality assurance activities include testing, code reviews, and validation processes.

The Importance of IT Project Management:

Now, let's delve into why IT project management is of paramount importance in the contemporary business landscape:

1. **Alignment with Business Objectives:** IT projects often have direct ties to an organization's strategic goals. Effective IT project management ensures that these projects align with the broader business objectives, such as enhancing customer experience, increasing efficiency, or expanding market reach.

2. **Resource Optimization:** IT projects typically involve significant investments in terms of time, money, and human resources. Proper management optimizes these resources, preventing wastage and improving the return on investment.

3. **Risk Mitigation:** The IT landscape is rife with uncertainties, from technical glitches to changing market conditions. IT project management involves thorough risk assessment and mitigation strategies, reducing the likelihood of project failure.

4. **Timely Delivery:** Meeting project deadlines is often critical in the fast-paced IT industry. Delays can lead to missed

opportunities and increased costs. IT project management techniques, such as critical path analysis, help ensure timely delivery.

5. **Cost Control:** Overspending is a common issue in IT projects. Project managers monitor budgets closely, making adjustments as needed to control costs and prevent financial crises.

6. **Quality Assurance:** In the IT sector, subpar quality can lead to system failures, security breaches, or user dissatisfaction. IT project managers focus on quality assurance processes to deliver reliable and high-performing solutions.

7. **Stakeholder Communication:** Effective IT project management involves clear and consistent communication with stakeholders, ensuring their needs and expectations are met throughout the project lifecycle.

8. **Competitive Advantage:** Successfully executed IT projects can provide organizations with a competitive edge. This might involve launching innovative products, streamlining operations, or enhancing customer interactions.

In conclusion, IT Project Management is the linchpin that enables organizations to harness the power of technology effectively. It ensures that IT projects are well-defined, well-executed, and well-aligned with strategic objectives, ultimately driving business success in the digital age. As we progress through this book, we will explore the intricacies of IT project management, from project initiation to closure, equipping you with the knowledge and tools needed to excel in this dynamic field.

B. The Role of IT Project Managers

In the complex and ever-evolving world of Information Technology (IT), effective project management plays a pivotal role in the success of IT initiatives. IT project managers serve as the linchpin that holds together the various components of a project, ensuring that it progresses smoothly, meets its objectives, and aligns with organizational goals. Let's dive in and explore the multifaceted role of IT project managers in greater depth.

1. Project Leadership and Vision:

- **Defining the Project Vision:** IT project managers are responsible for creating a clear and compelling vision for the project. They articulate the project's goals, objectives, and expected outcomes to the project team and stakeholders.

- **Setting Direction:** They establish a roadmap for the project, outlining the steps and milestones required to reach the project's destination. This involves defining project scope, schedules, and resource allocation.

- **Inspiring the Team:** Effective IT project managers motivate and inspire their teams to work towards a common goal. They foster a sense of purpose and commitment among team members.

2. Planning and Organization:

- **Detailed Project Planning:** Project managers meticulously plan every aspect of the project, from defining tasks and dependencies to allocating resources and budgeting. They create a comprehensive project plan that serves as a roadmap for execution.

- **Resource Management:** They identify the right mix of human and technological resources needed for the project and allocate them efficiently. Resource management includes hiring, training, and performance evaluation.

- **Risk Assessment and Mitigation:** IT project managers identify potential risks and develop strategies to mitigate them. This involves analyzing technical, logistical, and financial risks and creating contingency plans.

3. Communication and Collaboration:

- **Stakeholder Engagement:** Project managers establish and maintain effective communication with stakeholders, including clients, executives, team members, and external partners. They ensure that stakeholders are informed about project progress and address their concerns.

- **Team Collaboration:** IT projects often involve cross-functional teams. Project managers foster collaboration among team members with diverse skills and backgrounds, ensuring everyone works harmoniously towards project objectives.

- **Conflict Resolution:** Conflicts and disagreements can arise during project execution. Project managers mediate disputes, find solutions, and maintain a positive team atmosphere.

4. Execution and Monitoring:

- **Task Execution:** IT project managers oversee the day-to-day activities of the project. They ensure that tasks are completed on schedule, within scope, and according to quality standards.

- **Progress Tracking:** Project managers use various tools and techniques to monitor project progress. This includes comparing actual progress to the project plan, identifying variances, and taking corrective actions as needed.

- **Quality Control:** They are responsible for maintaining the quality of project deliverables. This involves conducting quality assurance activities, performing testing, and ensuring compliance with industry standards.

5. Risk Management and Adaptation:

- **Adapting to Change:** In the IT landscape, change is constant. Project managers must be flexible and ready to adapt to evolving requirements, technologies, and market conditions.

- **Risk Management:** Continual risk assessment and mitigation are vital. Project managers anticipate potential issues and take proactive measures to minimize their impact on the project.

6. Closure and Evaluation:

- **Project Closure:** Once the project objectives are achieved, project managers oversee the project closure phase. They ensure that all deliverables are met, and necessary documentation is completed.

- **Post-Project Evaluation:** IT project managers conduct a thorough post-project evaluation, including lessons learned. This helps improve future project management processes and outcomes.

In conclusion, the role of IT project managers is multifaceted and demanding. They are not only responsible for technical aspects but also for leadership, communication, risk management, and ensuring alignment with organizational goals. Their ability to navigate the complexities of IT projects while inspiring their teams is essential for the successful delivery of technology initiatives in today's fast-paced and competitive IT landscape. Effective IT project managers are the driving force behind innovation and digital transformation within organizations.

C. Key Challenges in IT Project Management

While Information Technology (IT) projects hold the promise of innovation, efficiency improvements, and competitive advantage, they also present a unique set of challenges for project managers. Navigating these challenges effectively is essential for the successful completion of IT projects. Let's delve into the key challenges faced in IT project management:

1. Rapid Technological Advancements:

- **Challenge:** The IT landscape evolves at an astonishing pace, with new technologies, tools, and frameworks emerging regularly. Keeping up with these advancements can be a significant challenge, as outdated technology can lead to project delays and inefficiencies.

- **Solution:** Project managers must stay updated with the latest industry trends and technological advancements. They should also build flexible project plans that can accommodate changes in technology during the project's lifecycle.

2. Scope Creep:

- **Challenge:** IT projects are susceptible to scope creep, where the project's scope expands beyond its original boundaries. This can lead to increased costs, delays, and project failure.

- **Solution:** To address scope creep, project managers must establish clear project scopes and change control processes. Any proposed changes should be thoroughly assessed for their impact on the project's timeline, budget, and objectives.

3. Resource Constraints:

- **Challenge:** Acquiring and retaining skilled IT professionals can be challenging. Resource shortages can result in delays, project bottlenecks, and increased competition for talent.

- **Solution:** Project managers should proactively identify resource constraints and work with HR and management to secure the necessary resources. Developing contingency plans, cross-training team members, and outsourcing can also help address resource shortages.

4. Complex Requirements:

- **Challenge:** IT projects often involve complex and dynamic requirements that are subject to change. Gathering and documenting these requirements accurately can be difficult, leading to misunderstandings and project rework.

- **Solution:** Implement robust requirements gathering and management processes. Engage stakeholders early and frequently to ensure a thorough understanding of their needs. Agile methodologies, with their focus on collaboration and adaptability, can also help address changing requirements.

5. Risk Management:

- **Challenge:** IT projects face various risks, such as technology failures, cybersecurity threats, and market fluctuations. Failure to address these risks adequately can lead to project setbacks or even failure.

- **Solution:** Project managers must conduct comprehensive risk assessments and develop risk mitigation strategies. This includes contingency planning, security measures, and regular risk monitoring throughout the project.

6. Stakeholder Management:

- **Challenge:** IT projects often involve numerous stakeholders with diverse interests and priorities. Managing these stakeholders' expectations, ensuring effective communication, and obtaining their buy-in can be challenging.

- **Solution:** Establish clear lines of communication with stakeholders and involve them in project decisions. Regularly update them on project progress and address any concerns promptly.

7. Integration and Compatibility:

- **Challenge:** IT projects may involve integrating new systems with existing ones or ensuring compatibility with a variety of platforms and devices. Ensuring seamless integration can be complex.

- **Solution:** Conduct thorough compatibility and integration testing. Engage experts in system architecture and design to ensure that the project components work harmoniously together.

8. Quality Assurance:

- **Challenge:** Ensuring the quality and reliability of IT solutions is critical, as failures can have severe consequences. However, comprehensive testing and quality assurance processes can be time-consuming and resource-intensive.

- **Solution:** Implement rigorous testing protocols, including unit testing, integration testing, and user acceptance testing. Automated testing tools can help streamline the quality assurance process.

9. Budget and Cost Control:

- **Challenge:** IT projects can be expensive, and cost overruns are a common challenge. Managing the budget effectively is crucial to project success.

- **Solution:** Establish a robust budgeting process and closely monitor project expenses. Be prepared to make adjustments if necessary, and communicate any budgetary constraints to stakeholders.

10. Change Management:

- **Challenge:** Implementing IT solutions often requires changes in organizational processes and culture. Resistance to change among team members and stakeholders can hinder project success.

- **Solution:** Develop a change management plan that includes training, communication, and support for those affected by the changes. Engage with stakeholders early to address concerns and gain their support.

In conclusion, IT project management presents a dynamic and challenging landscape. Addressing these key challenges requires a combination of technical expertise, effective communication, adaptability, and proactive risk management. By acknowledging and preparing for these challenges, project managers can increase the likelihood of delivering successful IT projects that meet business objectives and drive innovation.

D. The Value of Effective IT Project Management

Effective IT project management is the linchpin that holds together the complex world of Information Technology (IT). It provides substantial value to organizations by ensuring that IT projects are executed efficiently, on time, within budget, and in alignment with strategic objectives. Let's explore the significant value that effective IT project management brings to businesses and IT initiatives.

1. Efficient Resource Utilization:

- **Maximizing Human Resources:** Effective project management ensures that the right people with the right skills are assigned to specific tasks. This minimizes resource wastage and maximizes team efficiency.

- **Optimizing Budgets:** Project managers closely monitor project budgets, controlling costs and preventing overruns. This efficient budget utilization can lead to significant cost savings.

2. Timely Delivery:

- **Meeting Deadlines:** IT project managers develop detailed project schedules and use techniques like critical path analysis to ensure that milestones and deadlines are met. Timely project delivery can give organizations a competitive edge and allow them to capitalize on market opportunities.

- **Reducing Time-to-Market:** In industries where time-to-market is crucial, effective project management can accelerate product or service launch, enabling organizations to capture market share swiftly.

3. Risk Mitigation:

- **Identifying and Managing Risks:** Project managers conduct thorough risk assessments and develop risk mitigation strategies. This proactive approach minimizes the impact of potential risks and increases project success rates.

- **Adaptation to Change:** Effective project management also equips organizations to adapt to changing circumstances, such as shifts in market conditions or unexpected technical challenges.

4. Quality Assurance:

- **Delivering Reliable Solutions:** IT project managers implement robust quality assurance processes, including testing and validation. This results in the delivery of high-quality, reliable IT solutions that meet user requirements.

- **Reducing Post-Implementation Issues:** By ensuring quality throughout the project lifecycle, effective project management reduces the likelihood of post-implementation issues, system failures, or costly rework.

5. Alignment with Business Goals:

- **Strategic Alignment:** IT project managers work closely with business stakeholders to ensure that IT projects align with the organization's strategic objectives. This alignment ensures that IT investments contribute directly to the organization's success.

- **Enhancing Customer Satisfaction:** Projects that meet business goals and user expectations enhance customer satisfaction, loyalty, and retention.

6. Improved Communication:

- **Stakeholder Engagement:** Effective project management involves clear and consistent communication with stakeholders, including clients, executives, team members, and external partners. This fosters collaboration and trust.

- **Conflict Resolution:** Project managers mediate conflicts and disagreements, reducing tensions and maintaining a positive team atmosphere.

7. Scalability and Growth:

- **Scalable Solutions:** Effective project management considers scalability, allowing organizations to expand and grow without major disruptions to existing IT systems.

- **Innovation:** By managing IT projects effectively, organizations can drive innovation, develop new products and services, and gain a competitive edge in their respective industries.

8. Knowledge Transfer:

- **Preserving Knowledge:** IT project managers ensure that knowledge and expertise gained during a project are documented and transferred to the organization. This knowledge preservation supports long-term sustainability and future projects.

9. Enhanced Decision-Making:

- **Data-Driven Insights:** Effective project management often involves the collection and analysis of project data and metrics. This data provides valuable insights that can inform future decisions and optimize project management processes.

10. Competitive Advantage:

- **Market Leadership:** Organizations that consistently deliver IT projects successfully gain a reputation for reliability and excellence, positioning themselves as market leaders.

- **Adaptability:** Effective project management equips

organizations to adapt to changing market conditions, technology trends, and customer demands, ensuring their continued relevance and competitiveness.

In conclusion, the value of effective IT project management extends far beyond the successful completion of individual projects. It permeates throughout the organization, impacting resource utilization, strategic alignment, customer satisfaction, and the overall ability to innovate and grow. Recognizing and investing in effective IT project management is a strategic imperative for organizations seeking to thrive in the dynamic world of technology and business.

CHAPTER 2

Project Initiation: Paving the Path to Success

Project initiation marks the crucial starting point in the journey of any endeavor, setting the stage for what lies ahead. In the realm of project management, it is the moment when ideas take shape, goals are defined, and the path to success is charted. Whether you're embarking on a groundbreaking IT project, launching a new product, or implementing a strategic initiative, project initiation is the foundation upon which everything else is built.

In this chapter, we delve into the intricate art of project initiation, exploring its significance, key components, and best practices. We'll uncover the process of transforming a concept into a well-defined project, including the creation of project charters, the identification of stakeholders, feasibility studies, and the critical task of defining project scope. As we embark on this journey through project initiation, you'll gain insights into the essential steps that lay the groundwork for successful project management and execution. Welcome to the genesis of project excellence.

A. Project Charter and Objectives: The

Blueprint for Project Success

In the intricate landscape of project management, the project charter stands as a beacon, guiding the way from conception to completion. It serves as a foundational document that formally authorizes the existence of a project and provides the essential framework for its execution. Within this document, project objectives take center stage, serving as the North Star that aligns every project activity with the overarching goals. Let's delve into the depths of the project charter and objectives to understand their pivotal role in project success.

Project Charter: The Authorization Document

A project charter is the cornerstone of project initiation, acting as the official "birth certificate" of the project. It serves several crucial purposes:

1. Authorization and Recognition:

- **Challenge:** In the absence of a project charter, a project may lack formal recognition and authorization. This can lead to ambiguity, conflicting priorities, and difficulty in securing necessary resources.

- **Solution:** The project charter formally authorizes the project's existence, ensuring that it has the backing of key stakeholders and the organization's leadership.

2. Clarity of Purpose:

- **Challenge:** Without a clearly defined purpose, project teams may lose sight of the project's objectives, leading to misalignment and confusion.

- **Solution:** The project charter succinctly states the project's purpose, objectives, and anticipated benefits. It provides a common understanding of why the project is essential.

3. Scope Definition:

- **Challenge:** Scope creep, or the uncontrolled expansion of a project's boundaries, can lead to budget overruns and missed deadlines.

- **Solution:** The project charter outlines the project's scope, specifying what is included and what is excluded. It acts as a reference point to prevent scope changes without due consideration.

4. Stakeholder Identification:

- **Challenge:** Failing to identify and engage key stakeholders can result in inadequate support and feedback throughout the project lifecycle.

- **Solution:** The project charter identifies stakeholders and their roles, fostering engagement and ensuring that their interests are considered during project execution.

5. High-Level Milestones:

- **Challenge:** Lack of clear milestones can make it difficult to track progress and ensure that the project stays on schedule.

- **Solution:** The project charter often includes high-level milestones or deliverables, providing a roadmap for project execution.

Project Objectives: The Guiding Stars

Project objectives are the heart and soul of the project charter. They serve as the guiding stars that illuminate the path to project success. Key aspects of project objectives include:

1. Specificity:

- **Challenge:** Vague or unclear objectives can lead to confusion and misalignment among team members.

- **Solution:** Project objectives should be specific, measurable, achievable, relevant, and time-bound (SMART). This clarity ensures that everyone understands what needs to be accomplished.

2. Alignment with Strategic Goals:

- **Challenge:** Projects that are not aligned with an organization's strategic goals may fail to deliver meaningful value.

- **Solution:** Project objectives should be closely aligned with the broader strategic goals of the organization, ensuring that the project contributes to its mission.

3. Prioritization:

- **Challenge:** Projects often face constraints, such as limited resources or tight schedules. Failing to prioritize objectives can lead to resource allocation issues.

- **Solution:** Objectives should be prioritized based on their importance and impact on the project and organization.

4. Flexibility:

- **Challenge:** In a dynamic environment, objectives may need to adapt to changing circumstances.

- **Solution:** While objectives should be clear, they should also allow for flexibility and adjustment when necessary.

5. Consistency with Scope:

- **Challenge:** Objectives should be consistent with the project's scope to avoid conflicting expectations.

- **Solution:** The project charter ensures that objectives are aligned with the defined scope, preventing scope changes that could disrupt the project.

In conclusion, the project charter and objectives form the bedrock upon which a project is built. They provide clarity, direction, and authorization, setting the stage for successful project execution. By crafting a well-defined project charter with clear, SMART objectives, project managers create a roadmap that guides the project team towards its destination, ensuring that every action and decision contributes to the achievement of project goals.

B. Stakeholder Identification and Analysis: Navigating the Project Landscape

In the realm of project management, stakeholders are the compass that guides project success. Identifying and analyzing stakeholders are foundational steps in project initiation that can significantly impact the project's outcomes. These steps involve recognizing the individuals, groups, or organizations with a vested interest in the project and understanding their needs, expectations, and influence. Let's dive into the depths of stakeholder identification and analysis to appreciate their crucial role in project management.

Stakeholder Identification:

Stakeholder identification is the process of systematically

recognizing all parties who may be affected by or have an impact on the project. This encompasses a broad range of individuals and groups, both internal and external to the organization. Key aspects of stakeholder identification include:

1. Inclusivity:

- **Challenge:** Failing to identify all relevant stakeholders can result in overlooked concerns and unexpected challenges.

- **Solution:** Project managers must cast a wide net to ensure that no stakeholder, no matter how minor their involvement may seem, is left unacknowledged.

2. Internal and External Stakeholders:

- **Challenge:** Some stakeholders are internal to the organization, such as employees or management, while others are external, including customers, suppliers, regulators, and the community.

- **Solution:** The identification process should encompass all categories of stakeholders to create a comprehensive picture of the project's landscape.

3. Hierarchical Structure:

- **Challenge:** Organizations often have hierarchical structures, and it's essential to identify stakeholders at various levels of the organization.

- **Solution:** Stakeholders can be categorized based on their level of influence and interest in the project. This classification helps prioritize engagement efforts.

4. Stakeholder Mapping:

- **Challenge:** In large projects, it can be challenging to visualize the relationships and connections between stakeholders.

- **Solution:** Stakeholder mapping tools and techniques, such as influence-interest grids or power-influence matrices, help project managers understand the relative importance of each stakeholder.

Stakeholder Analysis:

Stakeholder analysis goes beyond identification, delving into the dynamics of stakeholder relationships, needs, and expectations. Key aspects of stakeholder analysis include:

1. Influence and Interest:

- **Challenge:** Not all stakeholders have equal influence or interest in the project, and failing to recognize this can lead to mismanagement of stakeholder relationships.

- **Solution:** Stakeholder analysis assesses the level of influence each stakeholder wields over the project and their degree of interest in its outcomes. This helps prioritize communication and engagement efforts.

2. Needs and Expectations:

- **Challenge:** Stakeholders often have diverse needs, interests, and expectations, which can be challenging to balance.

- **Solution:** Project managers must conduct interviews, surveys, or workshops to understand stakeholders' needs and expectations. This information informs the project's requirements and scope.

3. Communication Preferences:

- **Challenge:** Different stakeholders may prefer different modes of communication, making effective communication a significant challenge.

- **Solution:** Stakeholder analysis helps project managers tailor their communication strategies to meet the preferences of each stakeholder, ensuring that information reaches the right people in the right way.

4. Risk Assessment:

- **Challenge:** Stakeholders can pose both risks and opportunities to the project. Ignoring potential risks can lead to project delays or failures.

- **Solution:** Stakeholder analysis assesses the potential impact of each stakeholder on the project's success or failure, allowing project managers to develop risk mitigation strategies.

5. Engagement Strategy:

- **Challenge:** Engaging stakeholders effectively requires a tailored approach that considers their unique characteristics and interests.

- **Solution:** Based on the analysis, project managers can develop engagement plans that outline how and when to involve stakeholders throughout the project lifecycle.

6. Iterative Process:

- **Challenge:** Stakeholder dynamics can change over time, necessitating ongoing analysis and adjustment.

- **Solution:** Stakeholder analysis should be an iterative process, with regular updates to ensure that the project remains aligned with stakeholders' evolving needs and expectations.

In conclusion, stakeholder identification and analysis are integral to project management, as they lay the groundwork for effective communication, risk management, and project success. By recognizing the diverse interests and influences of stakeholders, project managers can navigate the complex landscape of project execution with precision, ensuring that the project not only meets its objectives but also garners support and satisfaction from all those involved.

C. Development: Paving the Path to Project Viability

In the realm of project initiation, feasibility studies and business case development serve as the gatekeepers that separate viable projects from those that should remain on the drawing board. These critical steps involve rigorous analysis and assessment to determine whether a project is worth pursuing. Let's delve into the depths of feasibility studies and business case development to understand their pivotal roles in project management.

Feasibility Studies:

Feasibility studies are comprehensive assessments of a proposed project's viability, considering its technical, financial, operational, and organizational aspects. The primary objectives of a feasibility study are to:

1. Assess Technical Feasibility:

- **Challenge:** Failing to evaluate the technical feasibility of a project can lead to insurmountable technical challenges during implementation.

- **Solution:** Technical feasibility assesses whether the necessary technology, resources, and expertise are available to execute the project successfully. It considers factors such as infrastructure, hardware, software, and compatibility with existing systems.

2. Examine Financial Feasibility:

- **Challenge:** Lack of financial feasibility analysis can result in budget overruns and financial distress for the organization.

- **Solution:** Financial feasibility evaluates the project's cost estimates, revenue projections, and potential return on investment (ROI). It considers factors such as budget constraints, funding sources, and financial risk.

3. Analyze Operational Feasibility:

- **Challenge:** Neglecting operational feasibility can lead to inefficiencies and challenges in project execution and ongoing operations.

- **Solution:** Operational feasibility assesses whether the project can be integrated smoothly into existing operations and processes. It considers factors such as workforce readiness, workflow adjustments, and potential disruptions.

4. Evaluate Organizational Feasibility:

- **Challenge:** A project that doesn't align with the organization's culture, values, or strategic goals may face resistance or lack support.

- **Solution:** Organizational feasibility evaluates the project's alignment with the organization's mission, values, and strategic objectives. It assesses whether the project has the necessary support from leadership and stakeholders.

5. Risk Assessment:

- **Challenge:** Neglecting to identify and assess risks can result in unforeseen issues that derail the project.

- **Solution:** Feasibility studies include a risk assessment to identify potential risks and uncertainties that may affect the project's success. Mitigation strategies are developed to address these risks.

6. Recommendations:

- **Challenge:** After conducting the analysis, it's essential to provide clear recommendations on whether to proceed with the project.

- **Solution:** Feasibility studies conclude with a set of recommendations based on the analysis. These recommendations may include a green light to proceed, modifications to the project, or a recommendation to halt the project.

Business Case Development:

A business case is a comprehensive document that presents a compelling argument for why a project should be undertaken. It builds on the findings of the feasibility study and outlines the project's strategic, financial, and operational rationale. Key aspects of business case development include:

1. Justification and Objectives:

- **Challenge:** Failing to provide a clear justification for the project can result in skepticism among stakeholders.

- **Solution:** The business case clearly articulates the project's objectives, benefits, and alignment with the organization's strategic goals. It answers the question of why the project is essential.

2. Cost-Benefit Analysis:

- **Challenge:** Without a robust cost-benefit analysis, it's challenging to demonstrate the project's financial viability.

- **Solution:** The business case includes a detailed cost-benefit analysis that compares the project's costs to the anticipated benefits. It quantifies both tangible and intangible benefits and calculates the project's ROI.

3. Alternative Solutions:

- **Challenge:** Focusing solely on one solution without considering alternatives can lead to suboptimal decisions.

- **Solution:** The business case explores alternative solutions or approaches to achieving the project's objectives. It compares these alternatives and justifies the chosen approach.

4. Risk Assessment and Mitigation:

- **Challenge:** Ignoring potential risks can undermine the credibility of the business case.

- **Solution:** The business case identifies and assesses risks, providing strategies and contingency plans to mitigate them. This demonstrates that potential challenges have been considered and addressed.

5. Implementation Plan:

- **Challenge:** A lack of a clear implementation plan can lead to confusion during project execution.

- **Solution:** The business case outlines a detailed implementation plan, including timelines, milestones, resource allocation, and responsibilities. It provides a roadmap for project execution.

6. Stakeholder Buy-In:

- **Challenge:** Gaining support from key stakeholders is essential for project success.

- **Solution:** The business case is crafted to address the concerns and interests of various stakeholders, aiming to secure their buy-in and support for the project.

7. Decision-Making:

- **Challenge:** Without a well-structured business case, organizations may struggle to make informed decisions about project investments.

- **Solution:** The business case provides decision-makers with the information they need to make an informed choice about whether to approve, modify, or reject the project.

In conclusion, feasibility studies and business case development are essential steps in project initiation that ensure that projects are well-founded, justifiable, and aligned with organizational goals. These processes require rigorous analysis, assessment, and documentation to provide a solid foundation for project success and to secure the necessary approvals and resources. By conducting thorough feasibility studies and building compelling business cases, organizations can make informed decisions about which projects to pursue, allocate resources effectively, and achieve their strategic objectives.

D. Risk Assessment and Initial Planning: Safeguarding Project Success

In the multifaceted world of project management, risk assessment and initial planning are twin pillars that fortify a project's foundation. These critical phases of project initiation involve a systematic analysis of potential risks and the development of strategies to mitigate them. Let's dive into the depths of risk assessment and initial planning to understand their crucial roles in ensuring the smooth trajectory of a project.

Risk Assessment:

Risk assessment is the process of identifying, analyzing, and evaluating potential risks that could impact a project's objectives. It forms the bedrock upon which risk management strategies are built. Key aspects of risk assessment include:

1. Risk Identification:

- **Challenge:** Failing to identify all potential risks can lead to unexpected issues during project execution.

- **Solution:** The risk identification phase involves brainstorming sessions, stakeholder consultations, and expert input to compile a comprehensive list of risks. Risks can be categorized as internal or external, technical, operational, financial, or strategic.

2. Risk Analysis:

- **Challenge:** Not all risks are of equal importance, and devoting resources to low-impact risks can be inefficient.

- **Solution:** Risk analysis assesses the likelihood and potential impact of each identified risk. Qualitative analysis uses scales like high-medium-low, while quantitative analysis assigns probabilities and monetary values to risks.

3. Risk Evaluation:

- **Challenge:** Determining which risks warrant attention and mitigation efforts is essential for effective risk management.

- **Solution:** Risk evaluation combines the results of risk analysis to prioritize risks based on their severity and potential impact on project objectives. This process determines which risks are "acceptable" and which require mitigation.

4. Risk Mitigation Strategies:

- **Challenge:** Identifying risks is only the first step; it's essential to develop strategies to mitigate or manage these risks.

- **Solution:** For each high-priority risk, project managers and teams develop risk mitigation strategies. These strategies could involve risk avoidance, risk reduction, risk transfer, or risk acceptance.

5. Contingency and Reserve Planning:

- **Challenge:** Risk mitigation strategies may not always eliminate risks entirely, necessitating the allocation of contingency reserves.

- **Solution:** Contingency and reserve planning involves setting aside additional resources, time, or budget to address unforeseen risks that may materialize during project execution.

Initial Planning:

While risk assessment focuses on identifying and managing risks, initial planning encompasses broader project planning activities that lay the groundwork for execution. Key aspects of initial planning include:

1. Scope Definition:

- **Challenge:** Lack of clarity in project scope can lead to scope creep and uncontrolled changes.

- **Solution:** Initial planning includes defining the project's scope, including objectives, deliverables, boundaries, and exclusions. This definition ensures that everyone involved has a clear understanding of what the project entails.

2. Work Breakdown Structure (WBS):

- **Challenge:** Large, complex projects can become overwhelming without proper decomposition into manageable tasks.

- **Solution:** The creation of a work breakdown structure involves breaking down the project into smaller, more manageable components, facilitating task assignment and tracking.

3. Resource Allocation:

- **Challenge:** Inefficient resource allocation can result in underutilization or overallocation of resources.

- **Solution:** Initial planning allocates resources such as personnel, equipment, and budget according to the project's needs, taking into account resource availability and constraints.

4. Project Schedule:

- **Challenge:** Without a well-defined project schedule, project progress may be chaotic, leading to delays.

- **Solution:** Project managers develop a detailed project

schedule, which includes task sequencing, dependencies, timelines, and milestones. This schedule provides a roadmap for project execution.

5. Budget Development:

- **Challenge:** Unclear budgeting can lead to budget overruns or misallocation of funds.

- **Solution:** Initial planning involves budget development, which outlines the estimated costs for each project activity. It also establishes cost baselines and provides a basis for monitoring and controlling project expenses.

6. Communication and Reporting:

- **Challenge:** Without a clear communication plan, stakeholders may be uninformed about project progress and issues.

- **Solution:** Initial planning includes the development of a communication plan that outlines how information will be shared with stakeholders, including frequency, channels, and responsible parties.

7. Risk Response Planning:

- **Challenge:** Risks identified during risk assessment require specific response plans to address them effectively.

- **Solution:** Risk response planning defines the actions that will be taken to mitigate or manage identified risks. It also allocates responsibilities and resources for executing these responses.

8. Quality Planning:

- **Challenge:** Inadequate attention to quality planning can lead to subpar project outcomes.

- **Solution:** Initial planning includes quality planning, which establishes quality standards, metrics, and processes to ensure that project deliverables meet specified quality criteria.

In conclusion, risk assessment and initial planning are pivotal phases in project initiation that prepare the project for success. Risk assessment identifies potential challenges and provides strategies to address them, while initial planning defines the project's scope, resources, schedule, and communication processes. By diligently conducting risk assessments and comprehensive initial planning, project managers set the stage for efficient and well-organized project execution, ultimately safeguarding the project's success and its ability to achieve its objectives.

E. Project Scope Definition: Charting the Boundaries of Success

In the intricate landscape of project management, the scope definition is akin to the project's compass, guiding its direction and determining the boundaries of success. It's the process of precisely defining what a project will and will not entail. Project scope definition plays a pivotal role in project initiation, laying the foundation for project planning, execution, and control. Let's explore the depths of project scope definition to understand its significance and key components.

Importance of Project Scope Definition:

1. **Clarity of Objectives:**

   - **Challenge:** Ambiguous project objectives can lead to confusion among team members and stakeholders.

   - **Solution:** Scope definition articulates the project's objectives in clear and concise terms, ensuring that everyone involved understands the project's purpose and goals.

2. **Resource Allocation:**

   - **Challenge:** Without a well-defined scope, resource allocation becomes challenging, leading to inefficiencies and potential budget overruns.

   - **Solution:** Scope definition helps identify the resources, including personnel, equipment, and budget, required for the project, facilitating efficient allocation and utilization.

3. Risk Management:

- **Challenge:** Undefined scope can result in scope creep, where uncontrolled changes to the project's boundaries introduce new risks.

- **Solution:** Clearly defined scope acts as a barrier against scope creep, reducing the likelihood of unmanaged changes that could jeopardize project success.

4. Stakeholder Expectations:

- **Challenge:** Misaligned expectations among stakeholders can lead to dissatisfaction and conflicts.

- **Solution:** Scope definition aligns stakeholder expectations by providing a common understanding of what the project will deliver.

5. Project Control:

- **Challenge:** Without a defined scope, project managers lack a basis for monitoring and controlling project progress.

- **Solution:** Scope definition establishes a baseline against which project performance can be measured, enabling effective control and decision-making.

Components of Project Scope Definition:

1. **Project Objectives:**

   - **Definition:** Clear and concise statements of what the project aims to achieve. Objectives should be specific, measurable, achievable, relevant, and time-bound (SMART).

2. **Deliverables:**

   - **Definition:** Tangible or intangible products, results, or outcomes that the project will produce. Deliverables should be well-defined and directly related to project objectives.

3. **Inclusions:**

   - **Definition:** Elements, features, or tasks that are explicitly part of the project. Inclusions specify what the project will encompass.

4. **Exclusions:**

   - **Definition:** Elements, features, or tasks that are explicitly not part of the project. Exclusions set boundaries and clarify what the project will not cover.

5. **Constraints:**

- **Definition:** Limitations or restrictions that impact the project's execution. Constraints can include budget limitations, resource constraints, regulatory requirements, and more.

6. **Assumptions:**

- **Definition:** Conditions or factors that are considered to be true but are not guaranteed. Assumptions should be documented to mitigate risks associated with their uncertainty.

Process of Project Scope Definition:

1. **Initiate Scope Definition:** The scope definition process begins during project initiation. Project managers, stakeholders, and subject matter experts collaborate to define the project's purpose and objectives.

2. **Gather Requirements:** This involves collecting and documenting detailed requirements from stakeholders. Requirements specify what the project should deliver and serve as the basis for defining scope.

3. **Create a Scope Statement:** The scope statement is a formal document that includes all the components of scope definition, such as objectives, deliverables, inclusions, exclusions,

constraints, and assumptions. It serves as a reference throughout the project.

4. **Review and Validate:** The scope statement is reviewed and validated with key stakeholders to ensure that it accurately reflects their expectations and needs.

5. **Baseline Scope:** Once validated, the scope statement is baselined, meaning that it becomes the agreed-upon and approved project scope. Any changes to the scope require formal scope change requests.

Challenges in Project Scope Definition:

1. **Incomplete Requirements:** Insufficient or vague requirements can lead to scope ambiguity and misunderstandings.

2. **Scope Creep:** Uncontrolled changes to project scope can result in scope creep, causing project delays and budget overruns.

3. **Lack of Stakeholder Engagement:** Failure to engage stakeholders in the scope definition process can result in misalignment of expectations.

4. **Overly Optimistic Assumptions:** Relying on unrealistic assumptions can lead to project risks and challenges.

5. **Scope Uncertainty:** In some projects, scope may be uncertain or evolving, making scope definition a continuous process.

In conclusion, project scope definition is a pivotal step in project management, ensuring that project objectives, boundaries, and expectations are clearly defined. It provides the necessary foundation for effective project planning, execution, and control. By diligently defining and documenting project scope, organizations can enhance project success rates, minimize risks, and foster alignment among stakeholders, ultimately paving the path to project success.

CHAPTER 3

Project Planning: The Blueprint for Success

Project planning stands as the bedrock upon which successful endeavors are built, whether in the realm of business, construction, technology, or any other field. It is the meticulous process of envisioning, organizing, and orchestrating every aspect of a project, from its inception to its fruition. In the journey of project management, planning serves as the compass, guiding teams through the complex maze of tasks, resources, and timelines toward the realization of their goals.

In this chapter, we embark on a comprehensive exploration of project planning, unveiling its profound significance, key components, and best practices. We will delve into the intricacies of defining project scope, creating detailed schedules, allocating resources, managing risks, and establishing communication frameworks. As we navigate the landscape of project planning, you will gain insights into the art of transforming concepts and objectives into actionable plans, setting the stage for the seamless execution of projects, no matter their size or complexity. Welcome to the realm of meticulous preparation, where the seeds of success are sown and nurtured.

A. Project Schedule Development: Mastering the Art of Time Management

In the realm of project management, time is a finite and invaluable resource. Project schedule development is the systematic process of creating a detailed timeline that outlines when project activities will occur, how long they will take, and how they relate to one another. It is an essential element of project planning that ensures efficient resource allocation, timely task completion, and overall project success. Let's explore the intricacies of project schedule development, including its importance, key components, and best practices.

Importance of Project Schedule Development:

1. **Time Management:** A well-crafted project schedule is the cornerstone of effective time management. It provides a structured framework for organizing project activities and deadlines.

2. **Resource Allocation:** Project schedules help in allocating resources, including personnel, equipment, and budget, efficiently. Resource conflicts and overallocation can be identified and resolved through scheduling.

3. **Task Sequencing:** The schedule defines the sequence in which project tasks should be executed, ensuring that dependencies and prerequisites are considered, and tasks are executed in a logical order.

4. **Communication:** Schedules serve as a communication tool for project teams and stakeholders. They provide a clear timeline for everyone involved, fostering alignment and understanding.

5. **Risk Management:** Identifying critical path activities and potential delays in the schedule allows project managers to proactively address risks and develop mitigation strategies.

Components of Project Schedule Development:

1. **Work Breakdown Structure (WBS):**

   - **Definition:** The WBS breaks down the project into smaller, more manageable work packages or tasks. It serves as the foundation for schedule development.

2. **Task Sequencing:**

   - **Definition:** Task sequencing determines the order in which project tasks must be executed. It identifies dependencies between tasks, such as finish-to-start, start-to-start, finish-to-finish, and start-to-finish.

3. **Task Durations:**

   - **Definition:** Task durations specify the amount of time required to complete each task. Durations should be estimated accurately based on historical data, expert judgment, or analogous projects.

4. **Resource Allocation:**

   - **Definition:** Resource allocation assigns the necessary resources, such as personnel, equipment, and budget, to each task. Resource availability and constraints are considered.

5. **Milestones:**

   - **Definition:** Milestones are significant events or points in the project timeline. They represent key achievements or deliverables and help track progress.

6. **Critical Path:**

   - **Definition:** The critical path is the longest sequence of tasks that determines the project's overall duration. Tasks on the critical path have zero slack or float, meaning any delay in these tasks will delay the project.

7. **Schedule Baseline:**

   - **Definition:** The schedule baseline is the approved version of the project schedule. It serves as a reference point for measuring project performance and deviations.

Process of Project Schedule Development:

1. **Define Activities:** The process begins with defining project activities based on the work breakdown structure. Each activity is described in detail and includes information about dependencies and constraints.

2. **Sequence Activities:** Activities are sequenced based on their dependencies and logical order. Task relationships are established, and the critical path is identified.

3. **Estimate Activity Durations:** For each activity, realistic duration estimates are made. These estimates consider historical data, expert judgment, and the availability of resources.

4. **Develop the Schedule:** Using software tools or manual methods, the project schedule is created. Gantt charts, network diagrams, or other visualization techniques may be used to represent the schedule.

5. **Resource Allocation:** Resources are assigned to tasks, taking into account resource availability and constraints. Resource leveling may be performed to resolve resource conflicts.

6. **Schedule Compression:** If the project timeline needs to be shortened, schedule compression techniques like crashing (adding resources) or fast-tracking (performing tasks in

parallel) may be applied.

7. **Review and Baseline:** The project schedule is reviewed with stakeholders and, upon approval, baselined. Any changes to the schedule require formal change control processes.

Challenges in Project Schedule Development:

1. **Uncertainty:** Estimating task durations accurately can be challenging due to uncertainty and unforeseen events.

2. **Scope Changes:** Changes in project scope can disrupt the schedule, necessitating adjustments and potential delays.

3. **Resource Constraints:** Limited availability of skilled resources can lead to resource conflicts and scheduling challenges.

4. **Complex Dependencies:** Projects with intricate task dependencies require careful sequencing and management to avoid bottlenecks.

5. **Communication:** Ensuring that all project stakeholders have access to and understand the schedule can be a communication challenge.

In conclusion, project schedule development is a fundamental aspect of project management that requires meticulous planning and attention to detail. A well-constructed schedule serves as a roadmap for project teams, guiding them through the project's execution phase. By accurately defining tasks, sequencing activities, estimating durations, and considering resource constraints, project managers can develop schedules that facilitate efficient project execution and contribute to project success.

B. Resource Allocation and Management: Maximizing Efficiency and Productivity

Resource allocation and management are vital components of effective project planning and execution. In the realm of project management, resources encompass not only physical assets like personnel, equipment, and budget but also intangibles such as time and expertise. Efficiently allocating and managing these resources can make the difference between project success and failure. In this comprehensive exploration, we will delve into the intricacies of resource allocation and management, including their importance, key considerations, and best practices.

Importance of Resource Allocation and Management:

1. **Optimized Utilization:** Efficient resource allocation ensures that resources are utilized to their maximum potential, minimizing waste and redundancy.

2. **Cost Control:** Effective resource management helps control project costs by allocating resources as needed and avoiding

overallocation or underutilization.

3. **Time Management:** Proper resource allocation ensures that tasks are completed within the specified timelines, contributing to project schedule adherence.

4. **Risk Mitigation:** Managing resource availability and conflicts proactively can mitigate risks associated with resource constraints and delays.

5. **Quality Assurance:** Adequate resource allocation ensures that the right skills and expertise are available when needed, contributing to the quality of project deliverables.

Key Considerations in Resource Allocation and Management:

1. **Resource Identification:** Identify the types of resources required for the project, including human resources, equipment, materials, and budget.

2. **Resource Availability:** Assess the availability of resources, considering factors like resource constraints, holidays, and other project commitments.

3. **Resource Allocation:** Assign resources to specific tasks or activities based on their skills, availability, and project requirements.

4. **Resource Leveling:** Resolve resource conflicts and overallocation by adjusting resource assignments or task schedules.

5. **Resource Tracking:** Monitor resource usage throughout the project to ensure that resources are being used effectively and efficiently.

Best Practices in Resource Allocation and Management:

1. **Resource Planning:** Develop a resource management plan that outlines how resources will be identified, allocated, and managed throughout the project.

2. **Resource Skill Matching:** Assign resources with the appropriate skills and expertise to tasks that align with their strengths.

3. **Resource Buffer:** Maintain a resource buffer to account for unexpected resource constraints or delays.

4. **Resource Contingency:** Develop contingency plans for critical resources to mitigate risks associated with their unavailability.

5. **Communication:** Establish clear communication channels for resource allocation and changes to keep stakeholders informed.

6. **Resource Optimization Tools:** Utilize resource management software or tools to assist in resource allocation and tracking.

Resource Allocation Models:

1. **First-Come-First-Serve (FCFS):** Resources are allocated based on their availability, with the first resource available assigned to a task.

2. **Round Robin:** Resources are allocated in a cyclic manner, ensuring equitable distribution.

3. **Priority-Based:** Resources are assigned based on task priorities, with higher priority tasks receiving resources first.

4. **Resource Smoothing:** Resources are allocated to tasks to ensure that resource utilization remains within predefined limits over time.

5. **Resource-Constrained Critical Path (RCCP):** Allocates resources to critical path tasks to optimize project duration.

Challenges in Resource Allocation and Management:

1. **Resource Constraints:** Limited availability of specific resources can pose challenges in meeting project requirements.

2. **Changing Requirements:** Scope changes or evolving project requirements may necessitate adjustments in resource

allocation.

3. **Resource Conflict Resolution:** Resolving conflicts when multiple tasks require the same resource can be complex and time-consuming.

4. **Overallocation:** Assigning more resources than available can lead to resource burnout and inefficiency.

5. **Resource Tracking:** Continuously monitoring resource utilization and adapting to changing circumstances can be demanding.

In conclusion, resource allocation and management are essential facets of successful project execution. Efficiently allocating resources, monitoring their utilization, and proactively addressing resource constraints contribute to on-time project delivery and cost control. By implementing best practices and resource allocation models, project managers can navigate the challenges associated with resource management and optimize resource usage, ultimately ensuring project success and stakeholder satisfaction.

C. Budgeting and Cost Estimation: Navigating the Financial Landscape of Projects

Budgeting and cost estimation are foundational elements of project management that are instrumental in ensuring a project's financial health and success. They involve the process of estimating, planning, and controlling project costs to achieve desired project objectives within defined financial constraints. In this comprehensive exploration, we will delve into the intricacies of budgeting and cost estimation, including their significance, key components, and best practices.

Importance of Budgeting and Cost Estimation:

1. **Financial Control:** Budgeting and cost estimation provide a framework for monitoring and controlling project expenditures, helping to prevent budget overruns.

2. **Resource Allocation:** Accurate cost estimation aids in the efficient allocation of resources, including personnel, equipment, and materials.

3. **Risk Management:** Identifying and assessing costs upfront allows for better risk management and contingency planning.

4. **Stakeholder Expectations:** Establishing a budget and cost estimates helps align stakeholder expectations regarding project costs.

5. **Decision-Making:** Project budgets and cost estimates play a crucial role in decision-making, helping organizations determine whether to invest in a project or explore alternative options.

Key Components of Budgeting and Cost Estimation:

1. **Cost Categories:** Break down project costs into categories such as labor, materials, equipment, overhead, and contingency.

2. **Cost Estimates:** Develop detailed cost estimates for each category, considering historical data, expert judgment, and market research.

3. **Budget Baseline:** Establish a budget baseline, which represents the approved budget for the project, including all cost estimates.

4. **Cost Control:** Implement cost control measures to monitor project spending and make adjustments as necessary to ensure adherence to the budget.

5. **Cost Tracking:** Continuously track actual costs against the budget to identify variations and take corrective actions when necessary.

Best Practices in Budgeting and Cost Estimation:

1. **Detailed Work Breakdown Structure (WBS):** Develop a comprehensive WBS that breaks down the project into smaller tasks, making it easier to estimate and allocate costs.

2. **Historical Data:** Utilize historical data from previous similar

projects as a reference for cost estimation.

3. **Expert Input:** Seek input from subject matter experts and experienced project managers when estimating costs for specialized tasks or projects.

4. **Contingency Planning:** Include contingency reserves in the budget to address unexpected costs and risks.

5. **Documentation:** Maintain detailed records of all cost estimates, budget changes, and actual expenditures for auditing and future reference.

Types of Cost Estimation:

1. **Analogous Estimating:** This method relies on historical data from similar projects to estimate costs. It is quick and less detailed but may be less accurate.

2. **Parametric Estimating:** Parametric models use statistical relationships between project parameters (e.g., cost per square foot) to estimate costs. This method is more accurate than analogous estimating.

3. **Bottom-Up Estimating:** In this detailed approach, costs are estimated for each work package or task, and then aggregated to create an overall project estimate. It is the most accurate but also the most time-consuming.

4. **Three-Point Estimating:** This technique involves estimating three values for each task: the most optimistic, most likely, and most pessimistic. These values are then used to calculate a weighted average estimate.

Challenges in Budgeting and Cost Estimation:

1. **Uncertainty:** Estimating costs accurately can be challenging, especially for complex projects with many variables.

2. **Scope Changes:** Changes in project scope can lead to cost adjustments and the need for re-estimation.

3. **Inflation and Market Fluctuations:** Economic factors and market fluctuations can impact the accuracy of cost estimates.

4. **Resource Constraints:** Limited availability of skilled resources can lead to cost increases or project delays.

5. **Budget Oversight:** Ensuring that project teams adhere to the approved budget can be a challenge, requiring diligent cost tracking and control.

In conclusion, budgeting and cost estimation are essential processes in project management that contribute to project success by providing financial clarity and control. Accurate cost estimation and budgeting help organizations make informed decisions, allocate resources efficiently, and manage project finances effectively. By implementing best practices and utilizing appropriate cost estimation methods, project managers can navigate the challenges associated with budgeting and cost estimation, ultimately ensuring the financial viability of their projects.

D. Quality Planning: Ensuring Excellence in Project Deliverables

Quality planning is a fundamental process in project management that focuses on defining the standards, processes, and activities necessary to achieve and maintain the desired level of quality in project deliverables. It involves a systematic approach to ensure that the project meets the specified quality requirements and objectives. Quality planning is not limited to product or service quality but extends to processes, documentation, and overall project management. In this in-depth exploration, we will delve into the intricacies of quality planning, including its significance, key components, and best practices.

Importance of Quality Planning:

1. **Customer Satisfaction:** Quality planning ensures that project deliverables meet or exceed customer expectations, enhancing satisfaction and trust.

2. **Risk Mitigation:** Identifying potential quality issues in advance allows for proactive risk mitigation, reducing the

likelihood of defects or rework.

3. **Cost Control:** High-quality deliverables reduce the need for rework or corrections, leading to cost savings.

4. **Reputation and Branding:** Consistently delivering high-quality projects enhances an organization's reputation and brand, attracting future clients or stakeholders.

5. **Compliance:** Quality planning helps ensure that projects adhere to industry standards, regulations, and best practices.

Key Components of Quality Planning:

1. **Quality Objectives:** Define clear and measurable quality objectives that align with project goals and stakeholder expectations. These objectives serve as benchmarks for evaluating project success.

2. **Quality Standards:** Establish specific quality standards or criteria that define what constitutes acceptable quality for project deliverables. These standards can be industry-specific or based on organizational guidelines.

3. **Quality Metrics:** Identify key performance indicators (KPIs) and metrics that will be used to measure quality throughout the project lifecycle. These metrics should be quantifiable and tied to quality objectives.

4. **Quality Processes:** Document the processes and procedures that will be followed to ensure quality at each stage of the project. This includes quality assurance (preventing defects) and quality control (detecting defects).

5. **Roles and Responsibilities:** Clearly define the roles and responsibilities of individuals or teams responsible for quality management, including who will perform quality checks and audits.

6. **Quality Assurance Plan:** Develop a quality assurance plan that outlines how quality will be ensured throughout the project. This plan includes activities, timelines, and responsibilities.

7. **Quality Control Plan:** Create a quality control plan detailing how quality will be monitored, measured, and verified during project execution. It specifies when and how inspections and testing will be conducted.

8. **Continuous Improvement:** Implement processes for collecting feedback, analyzing performance data, and making continuous improvements to enhance quality over time.

Best Practices in Quality Planning:

1. **Early Involvement:** Integrate quality planning from the project's inception to ensure that quality considerations are

incorporated into all aspects of planning and execution.

2. **Stakeholder Involvement:** Involve key stakeholders in quality planning to align their expectations and requirements with project objectives.

3. **Clear Communication:** Establish effective communication channels for reporting and addressing quality issues or deviations from quality standards.

4. **Training and Skill Development:** Ensure that project team members have the necessary skills and training to meet quality requirements.

5. **Documentation:** Maintain comprehensive documentation of quality plans, standards, processes, and performance data for auditing and reference.

Quality Assurance vs. Quality Control:

- **Quality Assurance (QA):** QA focuses on processes and activities that prevent defects and ensure that the project is following established quality standards and procedures. It is a proactive approach to quality management.

- **Quality Control (QC):** QC involves monitoring, measuring, and verifying project deliverables to ensure they meet specified quality standards. It is a reactive approach that aims to detect and correct defects.

Challenges in Quality Planning:

1. **Balancing Cost and Quality:** Striking the right balance between project cost and quality can be challenging, as higher quality may come with increased costs.

2. **Changing Requirements:** Adapting to changing project requirements while maintaining quality standards can be complex.

3. **Resource Constraints:** Limited resources, such as time or budget, may impact the ability to implement comprehensive quality measures.

4. **Subjectivity:** Assessing and defining quality can sometimes be subjective, leading to differing interpretations and expectations among stakeholders.

5. **Continuous Improvement:** Ensuring that lessons learned from quality monitoring and audits are incorporated into future projects can be a challenge.

In conclusion, quality planning is a critical component of project management that ensures that project deliverables meet or exceed expectations and standards. By defining quality objectives, standards, metrics, processes, and responsibilities, organizations can systematically incorporate quality into their project management approach. Implementing best practices and distinguishing between quality assurance and quality control helps organizations navigate the complexities of quality planning, ultimately leading to successful project outcomes and satisfied stakeholders.

E. Procurement and Vendor Management: Navigating the Supplier Ecosystem

Procurement and vendor management are integral aspects of project management that involve the strategic acquisition of goods, services, or resources from external suppliers or vendors. These processes play a crucial role in ensuring that a project has access to the necessary inputs and expertise to meet its objectives efficiently and cost-effectively. Effective procurement and vendor management can lead to successful project outcomes, while poor management can introduce risks and delays. In this in-depth exploration, we will delve into the intricacies of procurement and vendor management, including their significance, key components, and best practices.

Importance of Procurement and Vendor Management:

1. **Resource Acquisition:** Procurement enables projects to acquire external resources, including materials, equipment, and specialized skills, that may not be available internally.

2. **Cost Efficiency:** Effective procurement practices can lead to

cost savings through competitive bidding, negotiations, and economies of scale.

3. **Risk Mitigation:** Proper vendor selection and management can reduce the risk of supplier-related issues, such as delivery delays or quality problems.

4. **Expertise Access:** Projects can tap into the expertise and capabilities of specialized vendors, enhancing their ability to meet project requirements.

5. **Focus on Core Competencies:** Outsourcing non-core activities to vendors allows project teams to focus on core project tasks.

Key Components of Procurement and Vendor Management:

1. **Vendor Selection:** The process of identifying and evaluating potential vendors based on criteria such as capability, capacity, cost, quality, and past performance.

2. **Request for Proposal (RFP):** A document that outlines project requirements and solicits vendor proposals, including detailed information about the project, deliverables, timelines, and evaluation criteria.

3. **Contract Negotiation:** Negotiating the terms and conditions of the contract, including pricing, payment terms, deliverables,

warranties, and dispute resolution mechanisms.

4. **Supplier Relationship Management (SRM):** Ongoing management of vendor relationships throughout the project lifecycle, including communication, performance monitoring, and issue resolution.

5. **Quality Assurance:** Ensuring that vendor deliverables meet specified quality standards through inspections, testing, and audits.

6. **Risk Management:** Identifying and mitigating risks associated with vendor performance, including backup plans and contingency measures.

7. **Compliance:** Ensuring that vendors adhere to contractual and regulatory requirements, including ethical and legal considerations.

Best Practices in Procurement and Vendor Management:

1. **Clear Requirements:** Clearly define project requirements, objectives, and expectations in RFPs and contracts to minimize misunderstandings.

2. **Vendor Evaluation:** Conduct thorough due diligence when evaluating vendors, considering factors such as financial stability, reputation, and past performance.

3. **Competitive Bidding:** Encourage competition among vendors to obtain competitive pricing and favorable terms.

4. **Transparency:** Maintain open and transparent communication with vendors, addressing issues and changes promptly.

5. **Performance Metrics:** Establish key performance indicators (KPIs) to measure vendor performance and track progress.

6. **Vendor Collaboration:** Foster a collaborative relationship with vendors to leverage their expertise and address challenges proactively.

7. **Contract Management:** Implement robust contract management processes to ensure compliance with contractual terms and obligations.

Types of Procurement Contracts:

1. **Fixed-Price Contract:** A contract in which the vendor agrees to provide specific goods or services for a fixed price, regardless of the actual costs incurred.

2. **Time and Materials (T&M) Contract:** In this arrangement, the vendor is paid based on the time spent and the materials used to complete the project.

3. **Cost-Reimbursable Contract:** Under this contract, the

vendor is reimbursed for their allowable costs and may receive additional compensation for their performance.

4. **Incentive Contracts:** These contracts include performance incentives to motivate vendors to meet or exceed project objectives.

Challenges in Procurement and Vendor Management:

1. **Vendor Selection:** Identifying the right vendor can be challenging due to the need to balance cost, quality, and capability considerations.

2. **Contractual Disputes:** Contractual disagreements or disputes can lead to delays and increased costs if not resolved effectively.

3. **Performance Variability:** Vendors may not consistently meet performance expectations, leading to quality or schedule issues.

4. **Cultural Differences:** When working with international vendors, cultural differences in communication and business practices may present challenges.

5. **Data Security:** Protecting sensitive project data and intellectual property when working with external vendors is a significant concern.

In conclusion, procurement and vendor management are critical components of project management that require careful planning, execution, and ongoing monitoring. Effective procurement practices ensure that projects have access to the necessary resources and expertise while optimizing costs and managing risks. By implementing best practices, organizations can navigate the complexities of procurement and vendor management, fostering successful project outcomes and building strong, collaborative relationships with their vendors.

CHAPTER 4

Project Execution: Turning Plans into Reality

After meticulous planning and preparation, the project enters its most dynamic phase—project execution. This stage is the heartbeat of any project, where the carefully crafted plans and strategies are put into action. Project execution involves coordinating people, resources, and tasks to achieve project objectives, meet quality standards, and adhere to the established schedule and budget. It's the time when teams work collaboratively to bring a project to life, overcoming challenges and turning visions into tangible results. In this section, we embark on a comprehensive exploration of project execution, unraveling its significance, key elements, and best practices, all while navigating the dynamic landscape of project implementation. Welcome to the realm where plans become reality, and success is measured in action and achievement.

A. Team Building and Communication in Project Execution: The Pillars of Collaboration

In the realm of project execution, the effectiveness of a project team can make the difference between success and failure. Team building and communication are two interrelated pillars that underpin the collaborative efforts required to bring a project to fruition. These aspects of project management focus on forging a cohesive team, fostering open and effective communication, and promoting a positive working environment. In this in-depth exploration, we will delve into the intricacies of team building and communication, including their significance, key components, and best practices.

Importance of Team Building and Communication:

1. **Cohesive Team:** Team building fosters trust, respect, and cooperation among team members, resulting in a cohesive and motivated group.

2. **Efficient Workflow:** Effective communication ensures that information flows seamlessly within the team, preventing bottlenecks and misunderstandings that can hinder progress.

3. **Problem Solving:** Strong teams are better equipped to identify and address project challenges, fostering innovative solutions.

4. **Risk Mitigation:** Good communication helps in early identification and mitigation of risks, reducing the impact of potential issues.

5. **Stakeholder Engagement:** Effective communication extends to stakeholders, ensuring they are informed, engaged, and

aligned with project goals.

Key Components of Team Building:

1. **Team Formation:** Carefully select team members based on their skills, experience, and suitability for the project's objectives.

2. **Roles and Responsibilities:** Define clear roles and responsibilities for each team member to avoid confusion and overlap.

3. **Trust Building:** Foster trust and camaraderie among team members through team-building activities, open discussions, and shared experiences.

4. **Goal Alignment:** Ensure that every team member understands the project's goals and objectives, aligning their efforts with the project's vision.

5. **Conflict Resolution:** Develop conflict resolution mechanisms to address disagreements and disputes constructively.

6. **Recognition and Rewards:** Acknowledge and reward team members for their contributions and achievements.

Key Components of Communication:

1. **Clear Channels:** Establish clear communication channels for sharing project information, updates, and feedback.

2. **Regular Meetings:** Hold regular team meetings to discuss project progress, challenges, and upcoming tasks.

3. **Documentation:** Maintain comprehensive project documentation, including project plans, status reports, and meeting minutes.

4. **Transparency:** Promote transparency by sharing relevant project information with team members and stakeholders.

5. **Active Listening:** Encourage active listening within the team, where team members genuinely hear and consider each other's perspectives.

6. **Feedback Mechanism:** Create a feedback mechanism where team members can provide input and suggestions for improvement.

Best Practices in Team Building and Communication:

1. **Effective Leadership:** Strong leadership sets the tone for team building and communication. Leaders should lead by example, fostering a culture of trust and open communication.

2. **Diversity and Inclusion:** Embrace diversity within the team, as diverse perspectives can lead to more innovative solutions.

3. **Training and Skill Development:** Provide training and skill development opportunities to enhance team members'

communication and collaboration skills.

4. **Conflict Resolution Training:** Equip team members and leaders with conflict resolution skills to address issues constructively.

5. **Technology Tools:** Utilize collaboration and communication tools to facilitate remote or distributed team communication.

6. **Feedback Loops:** Establish feedback loops to continuously evaluate and improve team performance and communication.

Challenges in Team Building and Communication:

1. **Communication Gaps:** Communication breakdowns or misinterpretations can lead to misunderstandings and project delays.

2. **Cultural Differences:** In global or diverse teams, cultural differences in communication styles may pose challenges.

3. **Remote Teams:** Managing communication in remote or distributed teams can be challenging due to time zones and technology limitations.

4. **Conflict Handling:** Addressing conflicts and disagreements within the team can be complex and time-consuming.

5. **Resistance to Change:** Team members may resist changes in processes or communication methods.

In conclusion, team building and communication are fundamental aspects of project execution that empower project teams to work together cohesively, share information effectively, and overcome challenges. By implementing best practices, organizations can navigate the challenges associated with team building and communication, fostering a collaborative and productive environment that contributes to project success and stakeholder satisfaction.

B. Task Execution and Tracking: Driving Project Progress and Accountability

Task execution and tracking are pivotal components of project management, representing the practical implementation of project plans and ensuring that project activities progress as intended. Effective task execution involves the actual performance of project work by team members, while tracking encompasses monitoring, recording, and reporting on the status and progress of these tasks. Together, these processes ensure that project objectives are achieved on time and within scope. In this in-depth exploration, we will delve into the intricacies of task execution and tracking, including their significance, key elements, and best practices.

Importance of Task Execution and Tracking:

1. **Progress Monitoring:** Task tracking provides real-time

visibility into project progress, enabling project managers to identify delays or deviations and take corrective actions promptly.

2. **Accountability:** Task execution and tracking establish accountability within the project team, as team members are responsible for completing their assigned tasks on time.

3. **Resource Allocation:** By tracking task progress, project managers can allocate resources effectively and ensure that team members are optimally utilized.

4. **Quality Assurance:** Monitoring task execution allows for quality checks and validation to ensure that project deliverables meet quality standards.

5. **Risk Management:** Early identification of task-related issues facilitates risk mitigation and prevents potential project setbacks.

Key Components of Task Execution:

1. **Task Assignment:** Assign specific tasks to team members, clearly defining responsibilities, deadlines, and dependencies.

2. **Execution:** Team members perform the assigned tasks following established procedures and quality standards.

3. **Progress Reporting:** Team members regularly report on the

status of their tasks, highlighting any challenges or roadblocks.

4. **Issue Resolution:** Address issues or obstacles that may hinder task execution promptly, seeking solutions to minimize disruptions.

5. **Documentation:** Maintain records of task execution, including work logs, completion dates, and any changes made during execution.

Key Components of Task Tracking:

1. **Task List:** Create a comprehensive task list or schedule that outlines all project activities, their dependencies, and deadlines.

2. **Progress Updates:** Collect regular updates from team members regarding the status of their tasks, including percent complete, issues, and delays.

3. **Timeline Management:** Continuously monitor the project timeline to identify any tasks falling behind schedule or critical path issues.

4. **Resource Allocation:** Ensure that resources, such as personnel and materials, are allocated appropriately to support task execution.

5. **Quality Checks:** Verify that completed tasks meet quality

standards and are in accordance with project specifications.

6. **Risk Assessment:** Identify and assess risks associated with task execution and take proactive measures to mitigate them.

Best Practices in Task Execution and Tracking:

1. **Clear Task Descriptions:** Ensure that task descriptions are clear, concise, and include all necessary details to avoid misunderstandings.

2. **Regular Updates:** Encourage team members to provide regular updates on task progress, and establish a reporting frequency that suits the project's needs.

3. **Use of Technology:** Leverage project management software or tools to streamline task tracking and enhance visibility.

4. **Dependencies Management:** Clearly define task dependencies and monitor them closely to prevent bottlenecks.

5. **Key Performance Indicators (KPIs):** Define KPIs to measure task performance and project progress, using them as benchmarks for success.

6. **Feedback and Communication:** Foster open communication channels for team members to discuss challenges, propose solutions, and seek support.

Challenges in Task Execution and Tracking:

1. **Task Delays:** Unexpected delays or roadblocks can disrupt task execution and cascade into project delays.

2. **Resource Constraints:** Limited resources or unexpected resource shortages can hinder task execution.

3. **Scope Creep:** Uncontrolled changes in project scope can lead to additional tasks and complications.

4. **Data Accuracy:** Inaccurate or incomplete task updates can lead to incorrect project status reporting.

5. **Communication Breakdown:** Poor communication among team members can result in misunderstandings and misalignment.

In conclusion, task execution and tracking are vital components of successful project management, ensuring that project activities are carried out efficiently and progress is monitored effectively. By implementing best practices and addressing potential challenges, project managers can maintain control over project timelines, resources, and quality, ultimately leading to the successful achievement of project objectives.

C. Change Management in Project Execution: Navigating Organizational Transition

Change management is a critical component of project execution that addresses the processes, strategies, and actions needed to facilitate and manage transitions within an organization. During a project, changes are inevitable, whether they arise due to shifting project requirements, scope adjustments, technology upgrades, or shifts in stakeholder expectations. Effective change management ensures that these changes are introduced smoothly, minimizing disruptions and ensuring that the project's objectives are met. In this comprehensive exploration, we will delve into the intricacies of change management, including its significance, key components, and best practices.

Importance of Change Management:

1. **Smooth Transition:** Change management helps organizations transition from current practices or processes to new ones seamlessly.

2. **Minimized Resistance:** Properly managed change can reduce resistance from team members and stakeholders, making it easier to implement changes.

3. **Adaptability:** Change management fosters a culture of adaptability and resilience, essential in a dynamic business environment.

4. **Risk Mitigation:** Identifying and addressing potential issues or obstacles associated with change reduces the risk of project

disruptions.

5. **Improved Outcomes:** Effective change management can lead to improved project outcomes, including enhanced productivity and stakeholder satisfaction.

Key Components of Change Management:

1. **Change Identification:** Identify the need for change, whether it's a change in project scope, processes, technology, or stakeholder expectations.

2. **Change Impact Assessment:** Assess the potential impact of the proposed change on project objectives, scope, schedule, and resources.

3. **Change Planning:** Develop a comprehensive change management plan that outlines the strategies, activities, and resources required for change implementation.

4. **Stakeholder Engagement:** Engage stakeholders, including team members, sponsors, and end-users, to communicate the reasons for change and involve them in the change process.

5. **Communication:** Establish clear and consistent communication channels to share information about the change, its implications, and the timeline.

6. **Training and Development:** Provide necessary training and

development programs to equip team members with the skills required to adapt to the change.

7. **Resistance Management:** Identify and address resistance to change by acknowledging concerns, providing support, and facilitating dialogue.

8. **Monitoring and Evaluation:** Continuously monitor the progress of change implementation and evaluate its effectiveness in achieving the desired outcomes.

Best Practices in Change Management:

1. **Leadership Support:** Secure leadership buy-in and support for the change initiative, as the commitment of senior leaders can significantly impact change success.

2. **Early Communication:** Communicate the need for change early in the project, emphasizing the benefits and addressing concerns proactively.

3. **Change Champions:** Identify and empower change champions or advocates within the organization who can promote the change and support their peers.

4. **Feedback Loop:** Create a feedback mechanism for team members and stakeholders to express concerns, share ideas, and provide input on the change process.

5. **Incremental Change:** Whenever possible, implement changes incrementally, allowing individuals and teams to adapt gradually.

6. **Celebrate Milestones:** Recognize and celebrate milestones and achievements related to the change initiative to build morale and motivation.

Challenges in Change Management:

1. **Resistance:** Resistance to change is a common challenge, and addressing it effectively requires skill and patience.

2. **Uncertainty:** Change often brings uncertainty, and individuals may be anxious about the unknown.

3. **Overcoming Inertia:** Breaking established habits and routines can be difficult, and some team members may be resistant to changing their ways of working.

4. **Scope Creep:** Poorly managed changes can lead to scope creep, where the project's objectives expand without adequate control.

5. **Communication Breakdown:** Ineffective communication can lead to misunderstandings or incomplete information about the change.

In conclusion, change management is an essential aspect of

project execution that helps organizations navigate transitions and achieve project objectives successfully. By embracing best practices, addressing potential challenges, and fostering a culture of adaptability, organizations can proactively manage change, minimize disruptions, and increase the likelihood of successful project outcomes.

D. Risk Mitigation and Issue Resolution: Safeguarding Project Success

Risk mitigation and issue resolution are crucial components of project execution, dedicated to identifying, managing, and resolving potential risks and issues that can impact a project's progress and outcomes. Risk mitigation focuses on proactively reducing the likelihood and impact of anticipated risks, while issue resolution addresses problems that have already arisen during project execution. Together, these processes safeguard project success and enable teams to navigate challenges effectively. In this in-depth exploration, we will delve into the intricacies of risk mitigation and issue resolution, including their significance, key elements, and best practices.

Importance of Risk Mitigation and Issue Resolution:

1. **Project Continuity:** Risk mitigation prevents potential disruptions, ensuring that the project stays on course and remains within scope, schedule, and budget.

2. **Resource Optimization:** Effective issue resolution ensures that resources are used efficiently and that project teams can focus on productive tasks rather than troubleshooting.

3. **Stakeholder Confidence:** Successfully addressing risks and issues instills confidence in stakeholders, including sponsors, clients, and team members.

4. **Quality Assurance:** Mitigating risks and resolving issues helps maintain the quality of project deliverables and prevents costly rework.

5. **Cost Control:** Addressing issues promptly can prevent cost overruns resulting from delays or unexpected expenses.

Key Components of Risk Mitigation:

1. **Risk Identification:** Identify potential risks that could impact the project, considering internal and external factors.

2. **Risk Assessment:** Evaluate the probability and potential impact of identified risks, prioritizing them based on their significance.

3. **Risk Mitigation Strategies:** Develop strategies to reduce the likelihood or impact of high-priority risks, which may include risk avoidance, risk transfer, risk acceptance, or risk reduction.

4. **Risk Monitoring:** Continuously monitor identified risks

throughout the project lifecycle, reassessing their status and adjusting mitigation strategies as needed.

5. **Contingency Planning:** Develop contingency plans that outline actions to be taken if high-impact risks materialize.

Key Components of Issue Resolution:

1. **Issue Identification:** Identify and document issues as they arise, including their nature, impact, and potential root causes.

2. **Issue Prioritization:** Prioritize issues based on their potential impact on project objectives, timeline, and resources.

3. **Issue Resolution Plan:** Develop a resolution plan that outlines the steps, responsibilities, and timelines for addressing each issue.

4. **Issue Resolution Execution:** Implement the resolution plan, taking the necessary actions to resolve the issue and minimize its impact on the project.

5. **Issue Documentation:** Maintain detailed records of issue resolution efforts, including actions taken, outcomes, and any necessary follow-up steps.

Best Practices in Risk Mitigation and Issue Resolution:

1. **Proactive Risk Management:** Anticipate and address potential risks before they escalate into issues by

implementing proactive risk management strategies.

2. **Cross-Functional Collaboration:** Involve relevant stakeholders and subject matter experts in risk assessment and issue resolution efforts.

3. **Regular Reporting:** Provide regular updates to project stakeholders on the status of risk mitigation and issue resolution efforts, promoting transparency.

4. **Communication:** Maintain open and honest communication with team members and stakeholders throughout the process, ensuring that everyone is informed and aligned.

5. **Lessons Learned:** Capture lessons learned from risk mitigation and issue resolution to improve future project planning and execution.

6. **Documentation:** Thoroughly document all risk and issue-related information, as well as the actions taken to address them, for reference and audit purposes.

Challenges in Risk Mitigation and Issue Resolution:

1. **Incomplete Risk Identification:** Failure to identify all potential risks can leave the project vulnerable to unforeseen issues.

2. **Resource Limitations:** Limited resources, such as time or

budget, can constrain the ability to address risks and issues effectively.

3. **Scope Changes:** Scope changes can introduce new risks and issues, requiring adjustments to mitigation and resolution strategies.

4. **Stakeholder Expectations:** Managing stakeholder expectations regarding risk and issue resolution can be challenging, especially when there are delays or setbacks.

5. **Complexity:** Complex projects may have numerous interrelated risks and issues that require sophisticated mitigation and resolution strategies.

In conclusion, risk mitigation and issue resolution are integral to successful project execution, allowing teams to proactively manage potential challenges and address issues as they arise. By implementing best practices, maintaining open communication, and documenting all relevant information, organizations can navigate the complexities of risk mitigation and issue resolution, ultimately ensuring the achievement of project objectives and stakeholder satisfaction.

E. Stakeholder Engagement and Reporting: Ensuring Alignment and Transparency

Stakeholder engagement and reporting are vital aspects of

project execution that revolve around building and maintaining positive relationships with individuals or groups who have an interest in or are affected by the project. Effective stakeholder engagement fosters collaboration, helps manage expectations, and ensures that stakeholders remain informed and aligned with project objectives. Reporting, on the other hand, involves the regular and transparent communication of project progress, issues, and outcomes to stakeholders. Together, these processes contribute to project success and stakeholder satisfaction. In this in-depth exploration, we will delve into the intricacies of stakeholder engagement and reporting, including their significance, key elements, and best practices.

Importance of Stakeholder Engagement:

1. **Alignment:** Engaging stakeholders ensures that their interests, expectations, and requirements are aligned with project goals and objectives.

2. **Support:** Engaged stakeholders are more likely to provide the necessary support, resources, and buy-in for the project's success.

3. **Risk Mitigation:** Proactive stakeholder engagement helps identify potential issues or concerns early, allowing for timely resolution and risk mitigation.

4. **Decision-Making:** Engaged stakeholders can contribute

valuable input and insights to project decision-making processes.

5. **Stakeholder Satisfaction:** Effective engagement contributes to stakeholder satisfaction, which, in turn, can positively impact project outcomes and reputation.

Key Components of Stakeholder Engagement:

1. **Stakeholder Identification:** Identify all relevant stakeholders, including project sponsors, team members, clients, end-users, regulatory bodies, and other affected parties.

2. **Stakeholder Analysis:** Understand each stakeholder's interests, expectations, influence, and potential impact on the project.

3. **Communication Plan:** Develop a comprehensive communication plan that outlines how, when, and what information will be communicated to stakeholders.

4. **Engagement Strategies:** Tailor engagement strategies to the unique needs and interests of each stakeholder group, fostering collaboration and trust.

5. **Feedback Mechanisms:** Establish channels for stakeholders to provide feedback, raise concerns, and seek clarification throughout the project lifecycle.

6. **Issue Resolution:** Address stakeholder concerns and issues promptly, seeking mutually agreeable solutions.

Key Components of Reporting:

1. **Reporting Plan:** Develop a reporting plan that outlines the frequency, format, and content of project reports to stakeholders.

2. **Progress Reporting:** Regularly provide updates on project progress, including milestones achieved, timelines met, and challenges encountered.

3. **Issue and Risk Reporting:** Transparently communicate issues, risks, and their impact on the project, along with mitigation and resolution efforts.

4. **Quality Reporting:** Share information on the quality of project deliverables and adherence to quality standards.

5. **Financial Reporting:** Provide financial reports, including budget status, expenditures, and forecasts, to stakeholders as necessary.

6. **Resource Allocation:** Communicate resource allocation and utilization to ensure efficient use of resources.

Best Practices in Stakeholder Engagement and Reporting:

1. **Early Engagement:** Engage stakeholders early in the project

to gather input and set expectations from the outset.

2. **Customized Communication:** Tailor communication and reporting to the needs and preferences of different stakeholder groups.

3. **Consistency:** Maintain a consistent communication schedule and format to facilitate understanding and predictability.

4. **Two-Way Communication:** Foster open and two-way communication channels that allow stakeholders to voice concerns and provide input.

5. **Transparency:** Be transparent in reporting project status, issues, and challenges, even if the news is unfavorable.

6. **Regular Updates:** Provide regular updates to stakeholders, but avoid overwhelming them with unnecessary information.

Challenges in Stakeholder Engagement and Reporting:

1. **Diverse Stakeholders:** Managing the needs and expectations of diverse stakeholder groups can be complex.

2. **Conflicting Interests:** Balancing conflicting stakeholder interests can pose challenges in decision-making and prioritization.

3. **Resource Constraints:** Limited resources, including time and personnel, may hinder effective stakeholder engagement and

reporting efforts.

4. **Resistance:** Some stakeholders may resist engagement efforts or be reluctant to share information or concerns.

5. **Scope Changes:** Changes in project scope can affect stakeholder engagement strategies and reporting requirements.

In conclusion, stakeholder engagement and reporting are critical components of project execution that contribute to alignment, transparency, and project success. By implementing best practices and addressing potential challenges, organizations can foster positive stakeholder relationships, ensure informed decision-making, and maintain stakeholder satisfaction throughout the project lifecycle. This, in turn, enhances the likelihood of achieving project objectives and delivering value to stakeholders.

CHAPTER 5

Project Monitoring and Control: Guiding the Path to Success

In the dynamic landscape of project management, the ability to monitor progress, assess performance, and exercise control is essential for achieving project objectives efficiently and effectively. Project monitoring and control represent the vigilant oversight and management of a project's activities, resources, and outcomes, ensuring that it remains on track, within scope, on schedule, and within budget. These processes provide project managers with the data and insights needed to make informed decisions, mitigate risks, and adapt to changing circumstances. In this introductory exploration, we embark on a journey into the world of project monitoring and control, where vigilant scrutiny and strategic intervention guide the path to project success.

A. Project Metrics and Key Performance Indicators (KPIs): Navigating Project Success

Project metrics and Key Performance Indicators (KPIs) are indispensable tools in project management, serving as compasses to navigate a project toward success. They provide quantifiable, objective measures that enable project managers to monitor progress, assess performance, and make informed decisions. By collecting and analyzing data related to project activities, processes, and outcomes, project managers can identify areas for improvement, track project health, and ensure alignment with project goals. In this in-depth exploration, we will delve into the intricacies of project metrics and KPIs, including their significance, types, implementation, and best practices.

Importance of Project Metrics and KPIs:

1. **Performance Evaluation:** Metrics and KPIs provide an objective basis for evaluating project performance, enabling data-driven decision-making.

2. **Progress Tracking:** They help project managers track project progress, identifying delays, deviations, or areas where corrective actions are needed.

3. **Alignment with Objectives:** Metrics and KPIs ensure that project activities align with the overarching goals and objectives of the project and organization.

4. **Early Issue Detection:** By monitoring key indicators, project managers can detect issues or risks early, allowing for timely intervention.

5. **Stakeholder Communication:** Metrics and KPIs facilitate

clear and transparent communication with stakeholders, providing them with insights into project status.

Types of Project Metrics and KPIs:

1. **Time-Based Metrics:** These measure project progress in terms of time, including milestones achieved, task durations, and project schedule adherence.

2. **Cost-Based Metrics:** Metrics related to project budget, expenses, cost variances, and cost performance.

3. **Quality Metrics:** Indicators that assess the quality of project deliverables, adherence to quality standards, and defect rates.

4. **Scope Metrics:** Metrics that track changes in project scope, scope creep, and scope verification.

5. **Risk Metrics:** Metrics related to risk identification, risk impact, risk probability, and risk mitigation effectiveness.

6. **Resource Metrics:** Metrics assessing resource allocation, resource utilization, and resource availability.

7. **Stakeholder Satisfaction Metrics:** Metrics measuring stakeholder satisfaction and feedback, often gathered through surveys or feedback mechanisms.

Implementation of Project Metrics and KPIs:

1. **Identification:** Begin by identifying which project metrics and KPIs are most relevant to your project's objectives and stakeholders.

2. **Data Collection:** Establish data collection methods and sources for each metric or KPI. This may involve project management software, manual data entry, or automated data feeds.

3. **Baseline Establishment:** Set baseline values for each metric or KPI to provide a reference point for comparison throughout the project.

4. **Regular Monitoring:** Continuously monitor and collect data on project metrics and KPIs, updating them at regular intervals, such as weekly or monthly.

5. **Analysis:** Analyze the collected data to identify trends, patterns, and variations from baseline values.

6. **Actionable Insights:** Use the insights gained from the analysis to make informed decisions and take corrective actions when necessary.

7. **Communication:** Share the results of the metrics and KPI analysis with relevant stakeholders through reports or dashboards.

Best Practices in Project Metrics and KPIs:

1. **Alignment with Objectives:** Ensure that selected metrics and KPIs directly align with project objectives and organizational goals.

2. **Relevance:** Avoid collecting excessive data. Focus on metrics and KPIs that provide actionable insights and drive project improvement.

3. **Consistency:** Maintain consistency in data collection methods and reporting formats to enable meaningful comparisons.

4. **Real-Time Data:** Whenever possible, use real-time or near-real-time data for metrics and KPI analysis to enable timely decision-making.

5. **Benchmarking:** Compare project metrics and KPIs to industry benchmarks or historical data to gain additional insights.

6. **Continuous Improvement:** Use the insights from metrics and KPIs to drive continuous improvement in project processes and outcomes.

Challenges in Project Metrics and KPIs:

1. **Data Accuracy:** Ensuring the accuracy and reliability of data can be challenging, especially in manual data collection

processes.

2. **Selecting the Right Metrics:** Identifying the most relevant metrics and KPIs for a specific project requires careful consideration.

3. **Data Overload:** Collecting too much data can overwhelm project managers and stakeholders, leading to inefficiencies.

4. **Resistance to Measurement:** Team members or stakeholders may resist measurement efforts, viewing them as an additional burden.

5. **Changing Project Conditions:** Metrics and KPIs may need to be adjusted when project conditions change or new risks emerge.

In conclusion, project metrics and KPIs serve as invaluable guides on the journey to project success. When selected thoughtfully, implemented effectively, and analyzed judiciously, they empower project managers with the insights needed to make informed decisions, manage risks, and ensure that project outcomes align with organizational objectives. By adhering to best practices and addressing potential challenges, project managers can leverage these tools to drive continuous improvement and deliver successful projects.

B. Progress Monitoring and Reporting: Navigating Project Success

Progress monitoring and reporting are integral facets of effective project management, ensuring that projects stay on track, remain aligned with objectives, and provide stakeholders with transparency and accountability. These processes involve systematically tracking project activities, measuring performance against predetermined benchmarks, and communicating the status of the project to all relevant stakeholders. By doing so, project managers can identify issues early, make informed decisions, and take corrective actions when necessary. In this in-depth exploration, we will delve into the intricacies of progress monitoring and reporting, including their significance, key elements, best practices, and challenges.

Importance of Progress Monitoring and Reporting:

1. **Visibility and Transparency:** Progress monitoring and reporting provide stakeholders with a clear view of project status, fostering trust and confidence in project management.

2. **Alignment with Objectives:** These processes ensure that project activities and outcomes remain aligned with the project's goals, scope, and timeline.

3. **Issue Identification:** Monitoring allows for the early identification of issues, enabling timely intervention and risk mitigation.

4. **Decision Support:** Data from progress monitoring and reporting serves as the foundation for data-driven decision-making, helping project managers allocate resources and adjust strategies.

5. **Stakeholder Engagement:** Regular reporting keeps stakeholders informed and engaged, allowing them to provide feedback and make informed decisions.

Key Elements of Progress Monitoring:

1. **Performance Metrics:** Define specific performance metrics and key performance indicators (KPIs) that measure progress toward project objectives.

2. **Data Collection:** Establish a system for collecting relevant data, whether through manual input, automated tools, or a combination of both.

3. **Baseline Comparison:** Compare current progress to the project's baseline plan or initial schedule to identify variations.

4. **Regular Updates:** Continuously monitor and update progress data on a predetermined schedule, such as weekly or monthly.

5. **Documentation:** Maintain records of progress reports, including historical data, for reference and analysis.

Key Elements of Reporting:

1. **Report Format:** Define the format and structure of progress reports, ensuring they are concise, clear, and tailored to the needs of the audience.

2. **Frequency:** Determine how frequently progress reports will be generated and shared with stakeholders, considering the project's complexity and duration.

3. **Content:** Include relevant information in progress reports, such as milestones achieved, tasks completed, issues encountered, and future plans.

4. **Visual Aids:** Use visual aids, such as charts, graphs, and dashboards, to present data effectively and facilitate understanding.

5. **Narrative:** Provide a narrative that explains the data, highlights significant achievements or challenges, and outlines action plans.

Best Practices in Progress Monitoring and Reporting:

1. **Consistency:** Maintain a consistent schedule for progress updates and reporting to ensure stakeholders are well-informed.

2. **Clarity:** Use clear and straightforward language in progress

reports, avoiding jargon or overly technical terms.

3. **Audience-Centric:** Tailor progress reports to the needs and interests of different stakeholders, providing relevant details to each group.

4. **Action Orientation:** Include action plans and recommendations for addressing issues or variations in progress.

5. **Feedback Mechanism:** Encourage stakeholders to provide feedback on progress reports, fostering engagement and collaboration.

6. **Use of Technology:** Leverage project management software and tools for data collection, analysis, and automated reporting.

Challenges in Progress Monitoring and Reporting:

1. **Data Accuracy:** Ensuring the accuracy and reliability of progress data can be challenging, especially when relying on manual input.

2. **Scope Changes:** Changes in project scope can impact progress monitoring and reporting requirements.

3. **Resource Constraints:** Limited resources, including time and personnel, may hinder timely progress updates and reporting.

4. **Overwhelm:** Providing too much information in progress reports can overwhelm stakeholders, leading to information overload.

5. **Resistance:** Some stakeholders may resist progress monitoring and reporting efforts, viewing them as unnecessary bureaucracy.

In conclusion, progress monitoring and reporting are critical for steering projects toward success and keeping stakeholders informed and engaged. When executed with diligence and adherence to best practices, these processes ensure that project outcomes align with objectives, issues are addressed promptly, and transparency is maintained throughout the project lifecycle. By addressing potential challenges and tailoring reporting to stakeholder needs, project managers can effectively leverage progress monitoring and reporting to deliver successful projects.

C. Scope Change Management: Navigating Project Flexibility and Control

Scope change management is a vital process within project management that deals with the evaluation, approval, and control of changes to a project's scope. In the dynamic landscape of project execution, changes are inevitable. Stakeholder requirements evolve, unforeseen issues arise, and new opportunities emerge. Effective scope change management allows project managers to respond to these changes while maintaining control over the project's objectives, timeline, and budget. In this in-depth exploration, we will delve into the intricacies of scope change management, including its significance, key elements, best practices, and challenges.

Importance of Scope Change Management:

1. **Flexibility:** Scope change management provides the project with the flexibility to adapt to changing conditions, ensuring that evolving stakeholder needs are addressed.

2. **Risk Mitigation:** It helps identify and mitigate risks associated with changes, preventing potential disruptions to the project.

3. **Resource Allocation:** Effective management of scope changes ensures that resources are allocated efficiently to accommodate new requirements.

4. **Stakeholder Satisfaction:** Addressing scope changes promptly and transparently can enhance stakeholder satisfaction and build trust.

5. **Cost Control:** It helps control project costs by evaluating the impact of changes and making informed decisions regarding their approval.

Key Elements of Scope Change Management:

1. **Change Identification:** Establish a process for stakeholders to propose changes and document them thoroughly.

2. **Impact Assessment:** Evaluate the potential impact of each proposed change on project objectives, timeline, budget, and resources.

3. **Change Prioritization:** Prioritize changes based on their significance and alignment with project goals.

4. **Approval Process:** Define a clear and documented approval process for scope changes, including roles and responsibilities.

5. **Documentation:** Maintain detailed records of all scope changes, including their approval status, rationale, and impact assessment.

6. **Communication:** Communicate scope changes and their implications to all relevant stakeholders, keeping them informed.

Best Practices in Scope Change Management:

1. **Defined Change Control Process:** Establish a well-defined and documented change control process that outlines how scope changes are requested, evaluated, approved, and implemented.

2. **Change Request Form:** Require stakeholders to submit formal change request forms that include essential details such as the nature of the change, reasons, expected benefits, and impact assessment.

3. **Impact Analysis:** Conduct a thorough impact analysis for each proposed change to assess its effects on project scope, schedule, resources, and budget.

4. **Change Review Board:** Create a change review board or committee responsible for evaluating and approving scope changes to ensure objective decision-making.

5. **Change Log:** Maintain a comprehensive change log to track all proposed and approved changes throughout the project.

6. **Regular Reporting:** Include updates on scope changes in regular project status reports to keep stakeholders informed.

7. **Contingency Planning:** Develop contingency plans for high-impact changes to address potential risks and disruptions.

Challenges in Scope Change Management:

1. **Unclear Change Requests:** Incomplete or vague change requests can make it difficult to assess their impact accurately.

2. **Scope Creep:** Poorly managed scope changes can lead to scope creep, where the project's objectives expand without

adequate control.

3. **Resource Constraints:** Limited resources may hinder the project's ability to accommodate scope changes without impacting other project components.

4. **Stakeholder Expectations:** Managing stakeholder expectations regarding scope changes and their implications can be challenging.

5. **Decision-Making Delays:** Complex approval processes or indecision regarding scope changes can lead to delays and frustration among stakeholders.

In conclusion, scope change management is a fundamental process for maintaining project control while accommodating necessary changes. By implementing best practices and addressing potential challenges, project managers can effectively navigate scope changes, ensuring that they enhance project flexibility and contribute to successful project outcomes. Properly managed scope changes enable projects to adapt to evolving requirements while maintaining alignment with objectives and controlling potential risks.

D. Quality Assurance and Control: Ensuring Excellence in Project Deliverables

Quality assurance and control are integral components of

project management that focus on delivering high-quality outcomes while adhering to defined standards and objectives. These processes involve systematic planning, monitoring, and evaluation to ensure that project deliverables meet or exceed predetermined quality criteria. Quality assurance emphasizes proactive measures to prevent defects, while quality control focuses on detecting and rectifying defects in project work. In this in-depth exploration, we will delve into the intricacies of quality assurance and control, including their significance, key elements, best practices, and challenges.

Importance of Quality Assurance and Control:

1. **Stakeholder Satisfaction:** Delivering high-quality project outcomes enhances stakeholder satisfaction, trust, and confidence in project management.

2. **Risk Mitigation:** Quality assurance and control help identify and address potential risks and issues early, reducing the likelihood of costly rework or project failures.

3. **Resource Efficiency:** Ensuring quality throughout the project lifecycle minimizes resource wastage on fixing defects and rework.

4. **Compliance:** Meeting quality standards and regulatory requirements is essential, particularly in industries with strict compliance frameworks.

5. **Project Reputation:** High-quality deliverables enhance the project's reputation, positioning it positively within the organization and the industry.

Key Elements of Quality Assurance and Control:

1. **Quality Planning:** Define quality objectives, criteria, and standards that project deliverables must meet. Develop a quality management plan outlining how quality will be assured and controlled.

2. **Process Documentation:** Document project processes and workflows to ensure that they are repeatable and standardized. This includes defining roles, responsibilities, and procedures.

3. **Quality Metrics:** Establish measurable quality metrics and key performance indicators (KPIs) to assess project performance and the quality of deliverables.

4. **Quality Assurance (QA):** QA activities include process audits, reviews, and assessments to ensure that the project processes are being followed correctly. It focuses on preventing defects.

5. **Quality Control (QC):** QC involves inspecting and testing project deliverables to identify defects. It is the reactive aspect of ensuring quality and involves corrective actions.

6. **Defect Identification and Resolution:** When defects are

identified, a process should be in place for their timely resolution, which may include root cause analysis and corrective actions.

Best Practices in Quality Assurance and Control:

1. **Clear Quality Objectives:** Define clear and measurable quality objectives that align with project goals and stakeholder expectations.

2. **Early Detection:** Implement quality control measures early in the project to detect defects at the source and address them promptly.

3. **Continuous Improvement:** Foster a culture of continuous improvement by using lessons learned from quality control to enhance project processes.

4. **Training and Competence:** Ensure that project team members have the necessary training and competence to deliver high-quality work.

5. **Stakeholder Involvement:** Involve stakeholders in quality assurance and control processes, seeking their input and feedback.

6. **Documentation:** Maintain comprehensive records of quality control activities, including inspections, test results, and defect resolutions.

7. **Feedback Loop:** Establish a feedback loop that allows team members to report issues and improvements related to quality.

Challenges in Quality Assurance and Control:

1. **Resource Constraints:** Limited resources, including time and budget, can impact the thoroughness of quality control efforts.

2. **Scope Changes:** Changes in project scope can introduce new quality requirements and challenges.

3. **Complexity:** Complex projects may have numerous interrelated quality requirements and a higher risk of defects.

4. **Stakeholder Expectations:** Managing stakeholder expectations regarding quality can be challenging, particularly if they have varying definitions of quality.

5. **Overlooked Processes:** Inadequate attention to project processes can lead to defects in deliverables, even if the deliverables themselves meet quality criteria.

In conclusion, quality assurance and control are paramount in delivering project outcomes that meet or exceed expectations. By implementing best practices and addressing potential challenges, project managers can ensure that quality is ingrained in project processes and that deliverables are of the highest standard. This, in turn, contributes to stakeholder satisfaction, risk mitigation, and the overall success of the project.

E. Cost and Schedule Control: Balancing Project Resources and Timelines

Cost and schedule control are essential aspects of effective project management, focusing on the management and optimization of project resources and timelines. These processes aim to ensure that a project remains within its approved budget and adheres to its planned schedule. Cost control encompasses monitoring and managing project expenditures, while schedule control involves tracking and managing project timelines and milestones. In this in-depth exploration, we will delve into the intricacies of cost and schedule control, including their significance, key elements, best practices, and challenges.

Importance of Cost and Schedule Control:

1. **Budget Adherence:** Cost control ensures that a project stays within its budget constraints, preventing cost overruns that can strain resources and impact profitability.

2. **Resource Optimization:** Effective cost control enables efficient allocation and utilization of project resources, reducing waste and improving resource management.

3. **Timely Delivery:** Schedule control helps ensure that the project meets its milestones and deadlines, enhancing stakeholder satisfaction and trust.

4. **Risk Management:** Monitoring costs and schedules allows

for early detection and mitigation of potential issues and risks, reducing project disruptions.

5. **Stakeholder Confidence:** Adhering to budget and schedule commitments builds confidence among project stakeholders, including clients and team members.

Key Elements of Cost and Schedule Control:

1. **Budget Monitoring:** Regularly track project expenditures against the approved budget, including expenses for labor, materials, equipment, and overhead.

2. **Cost Analysis:** Conduct cost analysis to identify variances and deviations from the budget, enabling informed decision-making.

3. **Cost Forecasting:** Use historical cost data and trends to forecast future project expenses, helping to manage cash flow and resource allocation.

4. **Earned Value Management (EVM):** EVM is a technique that combines cost and schedule data to assess project performance and predict future outcomes.

5. **Change Control:** Implement a change control process to evaluate and approve changes that may impact project costs and schedules.

6. **Schedule Monitoring:** Continuously track project progress against the planned schedule, including milestones, deliverables, and critical path activities.

7. **Schedule Analysis:** Analyze schedule variances and delays to identify their causes and potential impact on the project's overall timeline.

Best Practices in Cost and Schedule Control:

1. **Baseline Establishment:** Create a project baseline that includes a well-defined budget and schedule, serving as a reference point for tracking and control.

2. **Regular Reporting:** Provide regular cost and schedule reports to stakeholders, highlighting variances and corrective actions.

3. **Variance Analysis:** Conduct in-depth variance analysis to understand the root causes of cost and schedule deviations and implement corrective measures.

4. **Change Management:** Implement a robust change management process to assess the impact of scope changes on cost and schedule.

5. **Resource Allocation:** Optimize resource allocation by aligning it with project priorities and critical path activities.

6. **Risk Assessment:** Identify potential risks and their impact on

cost and schedule, and develop mitigation strategies.

7. **Continuous Improvement:** Continuously refine cost and schedule control processes based on lessons learned from previous projects.

Challenges in Cost and Schedule Control:

1. **Resource Constraints:** Limited resources, including budget and skilled personnel, can pose challenges in effectively controlling costs and schedules.

2. **Scope Changes:** Changes in project scope can lead to cost and schedule variations if not managed properly.

3. **External Factors:** Economic fluctuations, supplier delays, and unforeseen events can impact project costs and schedules.

4. **Complexity:** Highly complex projects may have numerous interdependencies and variables that require sophisticated cost and schedule control measures.

5. **Stakeholder Expectations:** Managing stakeholder expectations regarding cost and schedule changes can be challenging, particularly if they have strict requirements or demands.

In conclusion, cost and schedule control are vital for project success, ensuring that projects are delivered within budget and on time. By implementing best practices and addressing potential challenges, project managers can effectively manage project resources and timelines, reduce risks, and build stakeholder confidence. These processes contribute to the overall success of the project and its ability to meet both financial and timeline objectives.

CHAPTER 6

Project Risk Management: Navigating the Uncertainties of Project Execution

Project risk management is an indispensable component of effective project management that focuses on identifying, assessing, mitigating, and monitoring risks that can impact a project's success. In the ever-changing landscape of project execution, uncertainties are omnipresent. These uncertainties, if not managed proactively, can lead to delays, cost overruns, and even project failure. Project risk management empowers project managers to anticipate potential issues, formulate strategies to address them, and ensure the project remains on course. In this introductory exploration, we embark on a journey into the realm of project risk management, where careful analysis and strategic planning guide the way through the challenges of project execution.

A. Risk Identification and Assessment: Safeguarding Project Success

Risk identification and assessment represent the foundational steps in the complex process of project risk management. These stages involve systematically identifying potential risks, analyzing

121

their likelihood and impact, and determining their significance to the project's objectives. Effective risk identification and assessment are critical for proactively managing uncertainties and avoiding potential setbacks. In this in-depth exploration, we will delve into the intricacies of risk identification and assessment, including their significance, key elements, methodologies, best practices, and challenges.

Importance of Risk Identification and Assessment:

1. **Proactive Management:** Identifying risks early allows project managers to take proactive measures to mitigate or manage them effectively.

2. **Objective Decision-Making:** Risk assessments provide data-driven insights that enable project managers to make informed decisions regarding resource allocation, contingency planning, and risk responses.

3. **Enhanced Stakeholder Confidence:** Demonstrating thorough risk assessment and management builds confidence among project stakeholders, as they can trust that potential issues have been considered and addressed.

4. **Resource Allocation:** By identifying and assessing risks, project managers can allocate resources more efficiently, directing them toward risk mitigation measures when necessary.

5. **Project Success:** Effective risk identification and assessment are key factors in preventing costly project delays, cost overruns, or failures, thereby contributing to overall project success.

Key Elements of Risk Identification and Assessment:

1. **Risk Identification:** Systematically identify potential risks that could impact project objectives, including internal and external factors.

2. **Risk Analysis:** Analyze identified risks to assess their likelihood of occurrence, potential impact, and significance to the project.

3. **Risk Prioritization:** Prioritize risks based on their assessed significance, allowing project managers to focus on the most critical threats.

4. **Risk Documentation:** Maintain a comprehensive record of identified risks, their characteristics, and the outcomes of risk assessments.

Methodologies for Risk Identification and Assessment:

1. **Brainstorming:** Conduct brainstorming sessions with project team members and stakeholders to generate a list of potential risks.

2. **Checklists:** Utilize predefined checklists or templates to systematically identify common project risks based on industry knowledge and best practices.

3. **SWOT Analysis:** Assess project strengths, weaknesses, opportunities, and threats (SWOT) to identify potential risks and opportunities.

4. **Root Cause Analysis:** Investigate historical project data and root causes of past issues to identify potential risks.

5. **Expert Judgment:** Seek input from subject matter experts who can provide insights into specific project risks based on their expertise and experience.

Best Practices in Risk Identification and Assessment:

1. **Cross-Functional Collaboration:** Involve a diverse group of project stakeholders, including subject matter experts, to ensure comprehensive risk identification.

2. **Regular Reviews:** Conduct periodic reviews of identified risks to account for changing project conditions and evolving uncertainties.

3. **Quantitative Analysis:** When possible, use quantitative methods to assess risk probability and impact, such as probability distributions and sensitivity analysis.

4. **Risk Register:** Maintain a risk register that includes detailed information about each identified risk, including its characteristics, potential consequences, and risk owner.

5. **Continuous Monitoring:** Continuously monitor identified risks throughout the project's lifecycle to detect changes in their status or new risks.

6. **Risk Tolerance:** Define risk tolerance thresholds to determine which risks require immediate attention and which can be managed with standard procedures.

Challenges in Risk Identification and Assessment:

1. **Biases:** Cognitive biases can influence risk perception and assessment, potentially leading to the underestimation or overestimation of certain risks.

2. **Incomplete Data:** Lack of historical data or incomplete information about potential risks can make accurate assessment challenging.

3. **Emerging Risks:** New risks may emerge during the project's execution that were not initially identified, requiring ongoing vigilance.

4. **Changing Environments:** External factors, such as regulatory changes or market shifts, can introduce new risks or alter the impact of existing ones.

5. **Subjectivity:** Risk assessments may be subjective, as different stakeholders may have varying opinions on the likelihood and impact of specific risks.

In conclusion, risk identification and assessment are foundational steps in effective project risk management. By following best practices and addressing potential challenges, project managers can proactively manage uncertainties, make informed decisions, and safeguard project success. Thorough risk identification and assessment set the stage for the development of robust risk response strategies, which can mitigate or exploit risks as the project progresses.

B. Risk Response Planning: Strategically Navigating Project Uncertainties

Risk response planning is a crucial phase in the project risk management process, following risk identification and assessment. This phase involves developing a well-thought-out strategy to address identified risks and uncertainties effectively. Risk response planning aims to mitigate, transfer, accept, or exploit risks to ensure that they align with the project's objectives and do not jeopardize its success. In this in-depth exploration, we will delve into the intricacies of risk response planning, including its significance, key elements, strategies, best practices, and challenges.

Importance of Risk Response Planning:

1. **Proactive Risk Management:** Risk response planning allows project managers to take proactive measures to address potential issues before they can impact the project negatively.

2. **Resource Optimization:** It enables efficient allocation of project resources by focusing efforts and resources on managing high-priority risks.

3. **Risk Mitigation:** Developing effective risk response strategies reduces the likelihood and impact of risks, minimizing disruptions to project progress.

4. **Stakeholder Confidence:** Demonstrating a well-considered approach to risk management builds stakeholder confidence in the project's ability to navigate uncertainties.

5. **Project Success:** Effective risk response planning contributes to successful project outcomes by ensuring that risks are managed in a controlled and strategic manner.

Key Elements of Risk Response Planning:

1. **Risk Mitigation Strategies:** Develop specific actions and plans to reduce the likelihood and impact of identified risks.

2. **Risk Acceptance Criteria:** Define under what conditions certain risks will be accepted without further intervention.

3. **Risk Transfer Approaches:** Determine how risks will be transferred to third parties, such as through insurance or contractual agreements.

4. **Risk Escalation Procedures:** Establish a process for escalating risks to higher levels of management or stakeholders when necessary.

5. **Contingency and Reserve Planning:** Develop contingency plans and allocate contingency reserves to address unexpected risks that may materialize.

Strategies for Risk Response Planning:

1. **Risk Mitigation:** Develop proactive strategies to reduce the probability or impact of risks. This may involve process improvements, additional quality control measures, or redundancy.

2. **Risk Avoidance:** Determine whether certain risks can be completely avoided by changing project plans, such as choosing a different technology or vendor.

3. **Risk Transfer:** Transfer risks to third parties through mechanisms like insurance, warranties, or outsourcing certain project components.

4. **Risk Acceptance:** Accept certain risks when their potential impact is low or when the cost of mitigation exceeds the

potential consequences.

5. **Risk Exploitation:** Exploit opportunities embedded in certain risks to gain competitive advantages or project benefits.

6. **Risk Sharing:** Collaborate with stakeholders or partners to share the impact and responsibilities of specific risks.

Best Practices in Risk Response Planning:

1. **Clear Ownership:** Assign clear ownership for each risk response strategy and ensure that responsible parties understand their roles.

2. **Monitoring and Tracking:** Continuously monitor the effectiveness of risk response plans and adjust them as needed based on changing circumstances.

3. **Contingency Planning:** Develop contingency plans for high-impact risks to ensure there are predefined actions in case they materialize.

4. **Documented Plans:** Maintain comprehensive documentation of all risk response plans and communicate them to relevant stakeholders.

5. **Integrated Approach:** Ensure that risk response plans are integrated into the overall project management plan and align with project objectives.

Challenges in Risk Response Planning:

1. **Resource Constraints:** Limited resources, including time and budget, can pose challenges in developing and implementing risk response plans effectively.

2. **Complexity:** Highly complex projects may have numerous interrelated risks, making it challenging to develop comprehensive and effective response strategies.

3. **Inadequate Data:** Lack of historical data or incomplete information about potential risks can hinder the development of effective response plans.

4. **Resistance to Change:** Stakeholders may resist changes to project plans or strategies, especially if they affect established processes or objectives.

5. **Overlooking Opportunities:** Focusing solely on risk mitigation may lead to missed opportunities embedded in certain risks that could have been exploited for project benefits.

In conclusion, risk response planning is a critical phase in project risk management that enables project managers to navigate uncertainties strategically. By implementing best practices and addressing potential challenges, project managers can develop robust response plans that align with project objectives, optimize resource allocation, and enhance stakeholder confidence. Well-considered risk response strategies contribute to successful project outcomes by ensuring that risks are managed in a controlled and proactive manner.

C. Risk Monitoring and Contingency Planning: Sustaining Project Resilience

Risk monitoring and contingency planning are essential components of project risk management that ensure project resilience in the face of evolving uncertainties. These processes involve continuous surveillance of identified risks, assessing their status, and executing predefined contingency plans when necessary. Effective risk monitoring allows project managers to detect changes in risk conditions, while contingency planning provides a structured approach to address risks that materialize. In this in-depth exploration, we will delve into the intricacies of risk monitoring and contingency planning, including their significance, key elements, best practices, and challenges.

Importance of Risk Monitoring and Contingency Planning:

1. **Dynamic Risk Landscape:** Projects operate in dynamic environments where risks can evolve or materialize unexpectedly. Risk monitoring and contingency planning ensure adaptability to changing conditions.

2. **Timely Intervention:** Early detection of changes in risk conditions enables project managers to take timely and informed action to prevent or mitigate potential issues.

3. **Resource Allocation:** Effective risk monitoring allows for efficient allocation of resources to manage risks that require immediate attention.

4. **Resilience:** Contingency planning ensures that predefined actions are ready for execution when risks materialize, reducing disruptions to project progress.

5. **Stakeholder Confidence:** Demonstrating proactive risk management builds stakeholder confidence by showcasing the project's preparedness for contingencies.

Key Elements of Risk Monitoring and Contingency Planning:

1. **Risk Monitoring:** Continuously assess the status of identified risks by tracking changes in their likelihood, impact, and overall significance.

2. **Contingency Plans:** Develop clear and documented contingency plans for high-impact risks, specifying actions, responsible parties, triggers, and communication protocols.

3. **Communication:** Maintain open and transparent communication with project stakeholders regarding risk

status, changes, and the execution of contingency plans.

Best Practices in Risk Monitoring and Contingency Planning:

1. **Regular Reviews:** Conduct periodic reviews of identified risks and their associated contingency plans to ensure relevance and effectiveness.

2. **Triggers and Thresholds:** Define specific triggers and thresholds that indicate when a risk has reached a critical point requiring contingency plan activation.

3. **Testing and Simulation:** Periodically test and simulate the execution of contingency plans to ensure readiness and effectiveness.

4. **Resource Allocation:** Allocate necessary resources, such as budget or personnel, to execute contingency plans promptly when needed.

5. **Documentation:** Maintain comprehensive records of risk monitoring activities, changes in risk conditions, and the execution of contingency plans.

6. **Integration:** Integrate risk monitoring and contingency planning into the overall project management framework to ensure alignment with project objectives.

Challenges in Risk Monitoring and Contingency Planning:

1. **Overlooked Risks:** The complexity of projects can lead to overlooked or underestimated risks, making it challenging to have comprehensive contingency plans.

2. **Resource Constraints:** Limited resources, including time and budget, can hinder the development and execution of contingency plans.

3. **Change Resistance:** Stakeholders may resist contingency plans or changes to project plans if they disrupt established processes or objectives.

4. **Complex Dependencies:** Risks in highly complex projects may have numerous interdependencies, making it challenging to manage them effectively.

5. **Complacency:** The absence of recent risk events can lead to complacency, causing project teams to neglect risk monitoring and contingency planning.

In conclusion, risk monitoring and contingency planning are vital for sustaining project resilience and ensuring successful outcomes in dynamic project environments. By implementing best practices and addressing potential challenges, project managers can proactively manage risks, detect changes in risk conditions, and execute well-defined contingency plans when necessary.

These processes contribute to the overall adaptability and resilience of the project, allowing it to navigate uncertainties and disruptions effectively.

D. Lessons Learned and Continuous Improvement in Project Management: A Path to Excellence

Lessons learned and continuous improvement are integral aspects of effective project management, emphasizing the need to reflect on project experiences, identify successes and challenges, and implement enhancements for future endeavors. These processes involve systematically capturing, analyzing, and applying insights gained from past projects to refine project management practices and increase project success rates. In this in-depth exploration, we will delve into the intricacies of lessons learned and continuous improvement in project management, including their significance, key elements, methodologies, best practices, and challenges.

Importance of Lessons Learned and Continuous Improvement:

1. **Knowledge Transfer:** Lessons learned facilitate the transfer of knowledge from one project to the next, enabling project teams to avoid repeating past mistakes and build on successes.

2. **Enhanced Efficiency:** Continuous improvement ensures that project management processes become more efficient over time, reducing waste and increasing productivity.

3. **Risk Mitigation:** Identifying and addressing recurring issues and challenges can mitigate risks in future projects.

4. **Stakeholder Satisfaction:** A commitment to continuous improvement demonstrates a commitment to delivering high-quality results, enhancing stakeholder satisfaction and trust.

5. **Competitive Advantage:** Organizations that embrace continuous improvement are better positioned to adapt to changing environments and maintain a competitive edge.

Key Elements of Lessons Learned and Continuous Improvement:

1. **Data Collection:** Systematically collect data and information from completed projects, including project documentation, reports, and stakeholder feedback.

2. **Analysis:** Analyze the collected data to identify patterns, trends, and recurring issues that require attention.

3. **Knowledge Sharing:** Share lessons learned and insights with relevant project teams, stakeholders, and the broader organization.

4. **Action Planning:** Develop action plans for implementing improvements based on the lessons learned and identified areas for enhancement.

5. **Implementation:** Execute the action plans and incorporate improvements into project management processes and practices.

Methodologies for Lessons Learned and Continuous Improvement:

1. **After-Action Reviews (AARs):** Conduct structured AARs at the conclusion of projects to assess what went well, what could have been improved, and how to apply lessons learned to future projects.

2. **Post-Project Reviews:** Systematically review completed projects to identify successes and challenges, document lessons learned, and determine areas for improvement.

3. **Benchmarking:** Compare project performance metrics and practices with industry benchmarks and best practices to identify areas for improvement.

4. **Surveys and Feedback:** Collect feedback from project team members, stakeholders, and clients through surveys and interviews to gain insights into project experiences.

Best Practices in Lessons Learned and Continuous Improvement:

1. **Dedicated Resources:** Assign dedicated resources or roles responsible for capturing, analyzing, and disseminating lessons learned.

2. **Formal Processes:** Establish formal processes for documenting and sharing lessons learned, including templates and repositories for easy access.

3. **Regular Reviews:** Conduct regular reviews of lessons learned and continuous improvement efforts, integrating them into project management routines.

4. **Actionable Insights:** Ensure that the lessons learned provide actionable insights and that improvements are specific, measurable, achievable, relevant, and time-bound (SMART).

5. **Knowledge Transfer:** Encourage knowledge sharing and mentorship within the organization to facilitate the transfer of lessons learned.

Challenges in Lessons Learned and Continuous Improvement:

1. **Lack of Time:** Project teams may prioritize current projects over documenting and analyzing lessons learned from completed ones.

2. **Resistance to Change:** Team members may be resistant to implementing changes based on lessons learned, especially if they disrupt established processes.

3. **Incomplete Data:** Inadequate documentation and data collection during project execution can hinder the identification of valuable lessons.

4. **Subjectivity:** Lessons learned can be subjective, influenced by individual perspectives and interpretations.

5. **Organizational Culture:** An organization's culture may not emphasize or support a culture of continuous improvement and knowledge sharing.

In conclusion, lessons learned and continuous improvement are critical for elevating project management practices and increasing project success rates. By following best practices and addressing potential challenges, project managers and organizations can create a culture of learning and improvement that drives excellence in project execution. Embracing the insights gained from past projects empowers project teams to make informed decisions, avoid common pitfalls, and ultimately achieve better results in future endeavors.

CHAPTER 7

Project Closure: The Culmination of Success and Learning

Project closure is the final phase in the project management lifecycle, marking the culmination of efforts, achievements, and lessons learned throughout the project journey. It involves systematically wrapping up project activities, ensuring that all objectives have been met, and formalizing the conclusion of the project. Project closure is not just about tying loose ends; it's an opportunity to celebrate successes, gather valuable insights, and transition smoothly to the next phase or project. In this introductory exploration, we embark on a journey into the world of project closure, where reflection, evaluation, and celebration play pivotal roles.

A. Project Acceptance and Deliverables Verification: Ensuring Stakeholder Satisfaction

Project acceptance and deliverables verification are critical components of the project closure phase, where the focus shifts from project execution to confirming that the project has achieved its objectives and met stakeholder expectations. This phase involves systematically reviewing project deliverables, ensuring they meet predefined criteria and standards, and obtaining formal acceptance from stakeholders. Effective project acceptance and deliverables verification not only validate project success but also build trust and satisfaction among stakeholders. In this in-depth exploration, we will delve into the intricacies of project acceptance and deliverables verification, including their significance, key elements, methodologies, best practices, and challenges.

Importance of Project Acceptance and Deliverables Verification:

1. **Stakeholder Satisfaction:** Confirming that project deliverables meet stakeholder expectations enhances their satisfaction and confidence in the project's outcomes.

2. **Legal and Contractual Obligations:** In contractual agreements, project acceptance often triggers payment or signifies the completion of contractual obligations.

3. **Risk Mitigation:** Verification helps identify any gaps or deviations in project deliverables, allowing for timely corrective actions and risk mitigation.

4. **Lessons Learned:** The process can uncover insights and lessons that can inform future projects and improve project management practices.

5. **Project Closure:** Successful project acceptance marks the formal conclusion of the project, allowing for a smooth transition to the next phase or project.

Key Elements of Project Acceptance and Deliverables Verification:

1. **Acceptance Criteria:** Define clear and measurable criteria that project deliverables must meet to be considered acceptable. These criteria are often outlined in project documentation or contracts.

2. **Verification Process:** Establish a systematic process for reviewing and verifying project deliverables, which may include inspections, testing, and validation against acceptance criteria.

3. **Stakeholder Involvement:** Engage relevant stakeholders, including clients, end-users, and project team members, in the verification process to ensure alignment with expectations.

4. **Documentation:** Maintain comprehensive records of the verification process, including the results, any deviations, and the actions taken to address them.

5. **Formal Acceptance:** Obtain formal acceptance from stakeholders once project deliverables have been verified and meet the acceptance criteria.

Methodologies for Project Acceptance and Deliverables Verification:

1. **Inspections:** Conduct systematic reviews of project deliverables to identify any defects or deviations from acceptance criteria.

2. **Testing:** Perform various forms of testing, such as functional, integration, or user acceptance testing, to validate that deliverables meet performance and functionality requirements.

3. **User Acceptance Testing (UAT):** Engage end-users or clients to test the deliverables in a real-world environment to ensure they meet user needs and expectations.

4. **Peer Reviews:** Utilize peer reviews or walkthroughs to gather feedback from project team members and subject matter experts.

Best Practices in Project Acceptance and Deliverables Verification:

1. **Clear Acceptance Criteria:** Ensure that acceptance criteria are well-defined, documented, and communicated to all stakeholders involved in the verification process.

2. **Transparency:** Maintain open and transparent communication with stakeholders regarding the verification

process, results, and any necessary corrective actions.

3. **Timely Verification:** Conduct verification activities promptly to address any issues or deviations as early as possible in the project closure phase.

4. **Comprehensive Documentation:** Maintain detailed records of the verification process, including the methods used, results, and any identified deviations.

5. **Alignment with Contracts:** Ensure that the verification process aligns with contractual agreements and obligations to avoid disputes.

Challenges in Project Acceptance and Deliverables Verification:

1. **Changing Requirements:** Evolving stakeholder requirements or expectations can pose challenges in achieving acceptance, requiring clear change management processes.

2. **Subjectivity:** Stakeholder perspectives on acceptance may vary, leading to disagreements that need to be addressed through effective communication and negotiation.

3. **Incomplete Deliverables:** In some cases, project deliverables may not be fully complete at the time of verification, requiring conditional acceptance with agreed-upon actions to address outstanding items.

4. **Resource Constraints:** Limited resources, such as time and budget, can impact the thoroughness and effectiveness of the verification process.

5. **Misalignment:** Misalignment between project teams, stakeholders, and contractual agreements can lead to confusion and delays in the acceptance process.

In conclusion, project acceptance and deliverables verification play a vital role in confirming that a project has met its objectives and satisfied stakeholder expectations. By following best practices and addressing potential challenges, project managers can ensure a smooth and successful project closure, enhancing stakeholder satisfaction, and facilitating a seamless transition to the next phase or project. Effective verification processes not only validate project success but also provide valuable insights that can inform future endeavors and continuous improvement efforts.

B. Transition Planning and Knowledge Transfer: Ensuring a Seamless Handover

Transition planning and knowledge transfer are essential components of the project closure phase, focusing on the smooth handover of project deliverables, responsibilities, and knowledge to relevant stakeholders. These processes ensure that the project's outcomes are effectively integrated into ongoing operations, maintenance, or further project phases. Transition planning also facilitates the transfer of critical project knowledge to individuals or teams who will continue to work with the project's results. In this in-depth exploration, we will delve into the intricacies of transition planning and knowledge transfer, including their significance, key elements, methodologies, best practices, and challenges.

Importance of Transition Planning and Knowledge Transfer:

1. **Seamless Operations:** Transition planning ensures that the project's deliverables are integrated into ongoing operations or subsequent project phases without disruptions.

2. **Knowledge Preservation:** Knowledge transfer preserves valuable project insights, best practices, and lessons learned for future reference and improvement.

3. **Sustainability:** Transition planning supports the sustainability of project outcomes by ensuring they continue to deliver value after the project's completion.

4. **Stakeholder Satisfaction:** Effective transition and knowledge transfer enhance stakeholder satisfaction by minimizing post-project issues and facilitating a smooth handover.

5. **Risk Mitigation:** A well-planned transition reduces the risk of project outcomes being underutilized or misunderstood by

stakeholders.

Key Elements of Transition Planning and Knowledge Transfer:

1. **Transition Plan:** Develop a comprehensive transition plan outlining the activities, timelines, responsibilities, and resources required for a successful handover.

2. **Stakeholder Engagement:** Engage relevant stakeholders, including end-users, operations teams, and support personnel, in the transition planning and knowledge transfer process.

3. **Knowledge Repository:** Create a repository or documentation system for storing project knowledge, lessons learned, and relevant documentation.

4. **Training and Capacity Building:** Provide training and capacity-building sessions to individuals or teams responsible for working with project outcomes.

5. **Documentation:** Document critical project information, processes, and procedures to ensure that it is accessible and understandable to future users.

Methodologies for Transition Planning and Knowledge Transfer:

1. **Structured Workshops:** Conduct workshops or collaborative

sessions to facilitate knowledge sharing and transfer among project team members and stakeholders.

2. **Documentation Review:** Review and update project documentation, ensuring that it is comprehensive and easily accessible to relevant parties.

3. **Mentoring and Coaching:** Pair experienced project team members with individuals who will assume responsibility for project deliverables to provide guidance and mentorship.

4. **Training Programs:** Develop training programs tailored to the specific needs of end-users or teams who will work with project outcomes.

Best Practices in Transition Planning and Knowledge Transfer:

1. **Early Planning:** Begin transition planning and knowledge transfer activities well before the project's closure to allow sufficient time for preparations.

2. **Tailored Approach:** Customize the knowledge transfer approach to the needs and preferences of the recipients, considering their existing knowledge and skills.

3. **Clear Communication:** Maintain clear and open communication with all stakeholders involved in the transition to ensure alignment and understanding of roles and

expectations.

4. **Knowledge Validation:** Verify that knowledge transfer has been successful by assessing the recipient's understanding and competence in working with project outcomes.

5. **Documentation Management:** Implement a structured and accessible documentation management system to store and retrieve project-related information efficiently.

Challenges in Transition Planning and Knowledge Transfer:

1. **Resistance to Change:** Stakeholders may resist adopting new processes or tools, leading to challenges in the transition.

2. **Time Constraints:** Limited time available for transition planning and knowledge transfer can impact the depth and effectiveness of these activities.

3. **Lack of Documentation:** Incomplete or outdated project documentation can hinder the knowledge transfer process.

4. **Knowledge Retention:** Ensuring that critical knowledge is retained and effectively transferred to future users can be challenging.

5. **Overlapping Responsibilities:** Clarifying roles and responsibilities in the transition process, especially in complex

projects, is crucial to avoid confusion.

In conclusion, transition planning and knowledge transfer are essential for ensuring the seamless handover of project outcomes and preserving valuable insights for future use. By following best practices and addressing potential challenges, project managers can facilitate a successful transition, enhance stakeholder satisfaction, and support the sustainability of project outcomes. Effective knowledge transfer processes not only enable stakeholders to utilize project deliverables effectively but also contribute to continuous improvement efforts and the organization's overall success.

C. Project Closure Documentation: Capturing the Legacy of Success

Project closure documentation is the final step in the project management lifecycle, where the comprehensive records, reports, and artifacts generated throughout the project are organized, reviewed, and formally archived. This documentation serves multiple purposes, including summarizing project achievements, assessing performance against objectives, capturing lessons learned, and providing a historical record for reference and compliance. In this in-depth exploration, we will delve into the intricacies of project closure documentation, including its significance, key components, best practices, and challenges.

Importance of Project Closure Documentation:

1. **Knowledge Preservation:** Documentation preserves the knowledge and insights gained during the project, ensuring that valuable lessons learned are not lost.

2. **Historical Record:** It creates a historical record of the project's activities, decisions, and outcomes, which can be essential for audits, compliance, and future reference.

3. **Evaluation and Assessment:** Closure documentation allows for an objective evaluation of the project's performance, enabling stakeholders to assess whether objectives were met and identify areas for improvement.

4. **Compliance and Reporting:** Some projects, especially in regulated industries, require formal documentation for compliance purposes and reporting to regulatory bodies or stakeholders.

5. **Communication:** It serves as a means of communicating project closure to all stakeholders, including team members, clients, and upper management.

Key Components of Project Closure Documentation:

1. **Project Summary:** A concise overview of the project, including its purpose, objectives, scope, and key milestones.

2. **Achievements and Deliverables:** A list of project achievements, completed deliverables, and a comparison against the initially defined scope and objectives.

3. **Performance Metrics:** Data and analysis related to project performance, including key performance indicators (KPIs) and metrics that measure the project's success.

4. **Lessons Learned:** Insights, best practices, challenges, and areas for improvement gathered from project experiences.

5. **Recommendations:** Suggestions and recommendations for future projects or initiatives based on lessons learned.

6. **Budget and Financial Summary:** A summary of project expenditures, cost variance analysis, and financial performance against the budget.

7. **Risk and Issue Log:** Documentation of risks and issues encountered during the project, their resolution, and any ongoing or unresolved items.

8. **Stakeholder Communications:** A record of all project-related communications, including meeting minutes, reports, and correspondence with stakeholders.

9. **Change Requests:** Documentation of all change requests, including their approval status and impact on the project.

10. **Closure Approval:** Formal approvals and sign-offs from key stakeholders indicating that the project has been successfully completed.

Best Practices in Project Closure Documentation:

1. **Start Early:** Begin documenting project closure activities well before the project's actual completion to ensure all necessary information is captured.

2. **Comprehensive Records:** Maintain detailed and comprehensive records throughout the project, making it easier to compile closure documentation.

3. **Standardized Templates:** Use standardized templates and formats for documentation to ensure consistency and ease of review.

4. **Cross-Functional Involvement:** Involve cross-functional team members, including project managers, subject matter experts, and financial experts, in preparing closure documentation.

5. **Validation and Verification:** Validate the accuracy of information included in the documentation and verify that it aligns with the project's objectives and outcomes.

Challenges in Project Closure Documentation:

1. **Incomplete Records:** Incomplete or missing documentation can hinder the preparation of comprehensive closure documentation.

2. **Time Constraints:** Limited time available for closure activities may result in rushed or incomplete documentation.

3. **Subjectivity:** Different stakeholders may have varying perspectives on project achievements and lessons learned, requiring effective communication and negotiation.

4. **Data Management:** Managing and organizing a vast amount of project data and records can be challenging without appropriate systems and tools.

5. **Stakeholder Engagement:** Ensuring that all relevant stakeholders provide input and approvals for closure documentation can be complex, especially in large projects.

In conclusion, project closure documentation is a vital component of the project management process, serving as a repository of knowledge and insights that can benefit future projects and provide transparency and accountability. By adhering to best practices and addressing potential challenges, project managers can ensure that closure documentation accurately reflects project achievements, lessons learned, and the legacy of success, ultimately contributing to organizational growth and continuous improvement efforts.

D. Celebrating Successes and Post-Implementation Review: Sustaining Achievements and Learning from Experience

Celebrating successes and conducting a post-implementation review (PIR) are crucial elements of the project closure phase that acknowledge achievements, recognize contributors, and facilitate learning from the project experience. While celebration serves as a morale booster and motivator, the PIR focuses on evaluating project performance, capturing lessons learned, and identifying opportunities for improvement. In this in-depth exploration, we will delve into the significance, key components, methodologies, best practices, and challenges of celebrating successes and conducting a post-implementation review.

Importance of Celebrating Successes:

1. **Motivation and Morale:** Celebrating successes acknowledges and rewards the hard work and dedication of the project team, boosting motivation and morale.

2. **Recognition:** It provides an opportunity to recognize individual and collective contributions, fostering a culture of appreciation and recognition.

3. **Team Bonding:** Celebrations promote team bonding and camaraderie, strengthening relationships among team members.

4. **Continued Engagement:** Positive recognition encourages team members to remain engaged and committed to future projects.

Key Components of Celebrating Successes:

1. **Acknowledgment:** Publicly acknowledge and thank all individuals who contributed to the project's success, including team members, stakeholders, and partners.

2. **Recognition:** Provide formal recognition, such as certificates, awards, or tokens of appreciation, to individuals or teams who made significant contributions.

3. **Celebratory Event:** Organize a celebratory event, such as a team dinner, award ceremony, or a simple gathering, to mark the project's success.

4. **Communication:** Share the project's achievements and successes with the wider organization to inspire and motivate others.

Best Practices for Celebrating Successes:

1. **Inclusivity:** Ensure that all team members, regardless of their

roles, are included in the celebration to foster a sense of unity.

2. **Tailored Recognition:** Personalize recognition to align with individuals' preferences and preferences, ensuring it resonates with each team member.

3. **Timely Celebration:** Hold the celebration shortly after project completion while the sense of achievement is still fresh.

4. **Continuous Appreciation:** Continue to acknowledge and appreciate contributions even after the celebration to sustain motivation.

Importance of Post-Implementation Review (PIR):

1. **Learning Opportunity:** The PIR provides a structured opportunity to learn from the project experience, both its successes and challenges.

2. **Continuous Improvement:** It identifies areas for improvement in project management processes, practices, and outcomes.

3. **Knowledge Capture:** Capturing lessons learned ensures that valuable insights and best practices are preserved for future reference.

4. **Accountability:** The PIR holds project managers and team

members accountable for achieving project objectives and outcomes.

Key Components of a Post-Implementation Review (PIR):

1. **Objectives Evaluation:** Assess whether the project achieved its stated objectives, and if not, identify the reasons and potential corrective actions.

2. **Performance Assessment:** Evaluate project performance against key performance indicators (KPIs), including cost, schedule, quality, and stakeholder satisfaction.

3. **Lessons Learned:** Document insights gained from the project, including successes, challenges, and recommendations for future projects.

4. **Stakeholder Feedback:** Gather feedback from project stakeholders, including clients, end-users, and team members, to understand their perspectives on project outcomes.

5. **Documentation Review:** Review project documentation, including plans, reports, and communication records, for accuracy and completeness.

Methodologies for Post-Implementation Review (PIR):

1. **Structured Workshops:** Conduct structured PIR workshops or meetings with project team members and stakeholders to

facilitate discussion and knowledge sharing.

2. **Surveys and Interviews:** Use surveys and interviews to gather feedback from a wider range of stakeholders, especially those who may not be directly involved in project management.

3. **Document Analysis:** Thoroughly review project documentation to identify patterns, trends, and areas for improvement.

Best Practices for Post-Implementation Review (PIR):

1. **Open and Honest Communication:** Foster an environment where team members feel comfortable sharing their experiences, both positive and negative.

2. **Actionable Insights:** Ensure that the PIR results in actionable insights and recommendations that can be applied to future projects.

3. **Cross-Functional Participation:** Involve individuals from different functional areas and roles to gain diverse perspectives.

4. **Structured Reporting:** Document PIR findings, recommendations, and action plans in a structured report for reference and future improvement efforts.

Challenges in Celebrating Successes and Conducting PIR:

1. **Time Constraints:** Limited time and resources may hinder the organization of celebrations and comprehensive PIRs.

2. **Subjectivity:** PIR findings and recommendations can be subjective and may vary among stakeholders.

3. **Resistance to Feedback:** Team members may resist providing negative feedback or acknowledging project shortcomings.

4. **Resource Allocation:** Allocating time and resources for PIR activities can be challenging, especially in busy project environments.

5. **Documentation Management:** Ensuring that project documentation is up-to-date and accessible for PIR can be a logistical challenge.

In conclusion, celebrating successes and conducting a post-implementation review are essential elements of project closure that contribute to motivation, continuous improvement, and knowledge preservation. By following best practices and addressing potential challenges, project managers can create a culture of appreciation, learning, and accountability within their teams and organizations. These processes not only recognize achievements but also pave the way for more successful and efficient future projects.

CHAPTER 8

Agile and Scrum in IT Project Management: Navigating the Dynamic Landscape

Agile and Scrum have revolutionized the world of IT project management by providing adaptable frameworks that embrace change and prioritize collaboration. In the realm of software development and IT projects, where requirements frequently evolve, Agile and Scrum offer methodologies that empower teams to respond flexibly to shifting priorities and deliver high-quality results efficiently. In this introductory exploration, we embark on a journey into the dynamic world of Agile and Scrum in IT project management, highlighting their significance, principles, methodologies, and benefits in navigating the ever-changing landscape of technology projects.

A. Agile Principles and Practices: The Foundation of Adaptive Project Management

Agile principles and practices form the bedrock of a project management philosophy that thrives in the face of complexity, uncertainty, and rapidly evolving requirements. Agile methodologies, with their origins in software development, have transcended their initial domain to become a guiding light for a diverse range of projects in IT and beyond. In this in-depth exploration, we will delve into the core principles and practices that underpin Agile project management, shedding light on their significance, key elements, methodologies, and benefits.

The Significance of Agile Principles and Practices:

1. **Adaptability:** Agile embraces change as a natural part of the project lifecycle, allowing teams to adapt to evolving requirements and priorities.

2. **Customer-Centric:** Agile focuses on delivering value to the customer early and often, ensuring that the end product meets customer needs.

3. **Collaboration:** Agile promotes collaboration and open communication among team members, stakeholders, and customers.

4. **Continuous Improvement:** Agile encourages continuous learning and improvement through regular reflection and adaptation.

5. **Transparency:** Agile methodologies emphasize transparency in project status, progress, and impediments, fostering trust and accountability.

Key Elements of Agile Principles and Practices:

1. **Iterative Development:** Agile projects are divided into small, manageable iterations or increments, with each iteration delivering a potentially shippable product increment.

2. **Customer Feedback:** Continuous feedback from customers and stakeholders guides the development process, ensuring that the project aligns with their needs.

3. **Cross-Functional Teams:** Agile teams are cross-functional, bringing together diverse skills and perspectives to work collaboratively on project tasks.

4. **Prioritization:** Agile teams prioritize work based on customer value, focusing on the most important features and tasks first.

5. **Self-Organization:** Agile teams have a degree of autonomy and self-organize to determine how best to achieve project goals.

Common Agile Methodologies and Practices:

1. **Scrum:** Scrum is one of the most popular Agile frameworks, emphasizing time-boxed iterations called "sprints," daily stand-up meetings, and well-defined roles like Scrum Master and Product Owner.

2. **Kanban:** Kanban is a visual project management approach

that focuses on visualizing work, limiting work in progress, and optimizing workflow.

3. **Extreme Programming (XP):** XP is a set of engineering practices within Agile, emphasizing practices like test-driven development (TDD), pair programming, and continuous integration.

4. **Lean:** Lean principles aim to reduce waste and improve efficiency, making it a valuable addition to Agile practices.

Benefits of Agile Principles and Practices:

1. **Faster Delivery:** Agile allows for faster time-to-market by delivering functional increments at the end of each iteration.

2. **Improved Quality:** Continuous testing and feedback in Agile lead to higher-quality products.

3. **Customer Satisfaction:** Agile's customer-centric approach ensures that the end product aligns with customer expectations.

4. **Risk Mitigation:** Agile's iterative nature allows teams to address risks and issues early in the project.

5. **Adaptability:** Agile's flexibility enables teams to pivot quickly in response to changing requirements or market conditions.

Challenges in Adopting Agile Principles and Practices:

1. **Cultural Shift:** Agile often requires a cultural shift within organizations, which can be challenging to implement.

2. **Customer Engagement:** Ensuring ongoing customer involvement can be difficult, particularly in large or distributed teams.

3. **Estimation:** Accurate estimation of work in Agile can be challenging, as requirements may evolve.

4. **Documentation:** Agile prioritizes working software over comprehensive documentation, which can be a shift for teams accustomed to extensive upfront planning.

5. **Team Collaboration:** Collaboration is crucial in Agile, and conflicts or communication issues can hinder progress.

In conclusion, Agile principles and practices have reshaped the landscape of project management, offering a dynamic and adaptable approach that resonates with the fast-paced world of IT and beyond. By embracing these principles and implementing Agile practices effectively, organizations can navigate complexity and change with confidence, deliver value to customers, and foster a culture of continuous improvement. Agile methodologies empower teams to thrive in an ever-evolving landscape, making them a cornerstone of modern project management.

B. Scrum Framework and Roles: Agile Collaboration for Effective Project Management

The Scrum framework is a widely adopted Agile methodology that provides a structured and iterative approach to project management. It is particularly popular in software development but has found applications in various other domains due to its flexibility and effectiveness. At the heart of the Scrum framework are defined roles, events, and artifacts that enable teams to work collaboratively, respond to change, and deliver value to customers. In this in-depth exploration, we will delve into the Scrum framework and its key roles, shedding light on their significance, responsibilities, and interactions.

The Scrum Framework:

Scrum follows a cyclical process composed of a set of defined events, roles, and artifacts, including:

1. **Scrum Events:** These are time-boxed activities that provide a cadence to the project. The core Scrum events include Sprint, Sprint Planning, Daily Scrum, Sprint Review, and Sprint Retrospective.

2. **Scrum Roles:** Scrum defines specific roles responsible for various aspects of the project. The key roles are the Product Owner, Scrum Master, and Development Team.

3. **Scrum Artifacts:** These are documents or information that provide transparency and shared understanding of project progress and objectives. The primary Scrum artifacts are the Product Backlog, Sprint Backlog, and Increment.

Key Roles in the Scrum Framework:

1. **Product Owner:**

   - **Significance:** The Product Owner represents the customer, end-users, and stakeholders, ensuring that the product delivers maximum value.

   - **Responsibilities:**

     - Defines and prioritizes items in the Product Backlog.

     - Represents the voice of the customer and conveys the product vision to the Development Team.

     - Makes decisions on what gets built in each Sprint.

     - Accepts or rejects work results based on predefined acceptance criteria.

2. **Scrum Master:**

- **Significance:** The Scrum Master acts as a servant-leader, ensuring that the Scrum framework is understood and followed while removing impediments and facilitating collaboration.

- **Responsibilities:**

  - Facilitates Scrum events, including Sprint Planning, Daily Scrum, Sprint Review, and Sprint Retrospective.

  - Shields the team from external disruptions and distractions.

  - Helps the team improve by promoting self-organization and continuous improvement.

  - Removes obstacles that hinder the team's progress.

3. **Development Team:**

- **Significance:** The Development Team is responsible for delivering a potentially shippable product increment during each Sprint.

- **Responsibilities:**

  - Collaborates with the Product Owner to understand and refine the items in the Product Backlog.

  - Self-organizes to determine how to best accomplish the work in each Sprint.

  - Holds each other accountable for delivering high-quality work.

  - Regularly inspects progress during the Daily Scrum and adapts their plan accordingly.

Interactions and Collaboration in Scrum:

The Scrum framework emphasizes collaboration among the roles to achieve project goals:

1. **Product Owner and Development Team:** Continuous collaboration between the Product Owner and Development Team ensures that the product backlog items are well-understood, and the team can work effectively toward achieving the Sprint goal.

2. **Development Team and Scrum Master:** The Development Team collaborates with the Scrum Master to address impediments and continuously improve their processes,

removing any obstacles that may hinder their progress.

3. **Scrum Master and Product Owner:** The Scrum Master assists the Product Owner in refining the product backlog, ensuring it is prioritized and refined effectively to meet customer needs.

4. **Development Team, Scrum Master, and Product Owner:** The Daily Scrum is a daily meeting where these roles collaborate to inspect progress and adapt their plan for the day.

Benefits of the Scrum Framework and Roles:

1. **Transparency:** The Scrum framework provides transparency into project progress, objectives, and obstacles through regular events and artifacts.

2. **Flexibility:** Scrum's iterative approach allows teams to adapt to changing requirements and priorities.

3. **Focus on Value:** Scrum prioritizes the delivery of value to customers, ensuring that the most valuable work is completed first.

4. **Accountability:** Clear roles and responsibilities help ensure that everyone knows their role in the project.

Challenges in Implementing the Scrum Framework and Roles:

1. **Cultural Shift:** Transitioning to Scrum may require a cultural shift within organizations accustomed to traditional project management approaches.

2. **Role Clarity:** Ensuring that each role understands its responsibilities and collaborates effectively can be challenging.

3. **Time-Boxed Events:** Meeting the time constraints of Scrum events, particularly in large projects, can be demanding.

4. **Scope Changes:** Handling changes in scope or requirements during a Sprint can be complex.

In conclusion, the Scrum framework and its key roles provide a structured yet flexible approach to Agile project management. By understanding the significance and responsibilities of each role and fostering collaboration, teams can leverage Scrum to adapt to change, deliver value, and continuously improve their processes. Scrum's emphasis on transparency, customer focus, and accountability makes it a valuable methodology for projects in IT and beyond.

C. Implementing Agile in IT Projects: A Framework for Success

Implementing Agile methodologies in IT projects has become increasingly prevalent as organizations seek more adaptive, customer-centric, and efficient approaches to delivering technology solutions. Agile, with its iterative and collaborative principles, offers a framework that allows IT teams to respond quickly to changing requirements and market dynamics while ensuring customer satisfaction. In this in-depth exploration, we will delve into the key aspects of implementing Agile in IT projects, including its significance, steps, best practices, and challenges.

The Significance of Implementing Agile in IT Projects:

1. **Adaptability:** Agile methodologies enable IT teams to embrace change as a natural part of the project, ensuring that evolving requirements are accommodated.

2. **Customer Focus:** Agile places a strong emphasis on understanding and meeting customer needs, resulting in solutions that align more closely with user expectations.

3. **Efficiency:** Agile practices, such as short iterations and regular feedback, promote efficient development and reduce the risk of wasted effort on features that aren't valuable.

4. **Quality:** Agile's iterative approach includes continuous

testing and validation, resulting in higher-quality software and fewer defects.

5. **Collaboration:** Agile encourages close collaboration among cross-functional teams, fostering better communication and a shared sense of responsibility.

Steps for Implementing Agile in IT Projects:

1. **Assess Current Practices:**

   - Evaluate existing project management methodologies, processes, and team dynamics to identify areas that can benefit from Agile.

2. **Training and Education:**

   - Provide Agile training and education to team members and stakeholders to ensure everyone understands the principles, practices, and roles involved.

3. **Select an Agile Methodology:**

   - Choose the most suitable Agile framework for your IT project, such as Scrum, Kanban, or Extreme Programming (XP).

4. **Form Agile Teams:**

   - Organize cross-functional Agile teams, including a

Product Owner, Scrum Master (if using Scrum), and Development Team.

5. **Adopt Agile Practices:**

   - Introduce Agile practices, including iterative development, short cycles (Sprints), daily stand-up meetings, and continuous integration.

6. **Create Backlogs:**

   - Develop a Product Backlog to capture all project requirements, and a Sprint Backlog for each iteration's tasks.

7. **Prioritize Work:**

   - Collaborate with the Product Owner to prioritize items in the Product Backlog based on customer value.

8. **Execute Sprints:**

   - Conduct Sprints, with the Development Team working on prioritized tasks and delivering potentially shippable increments at the end of each cycle.

9. **Feedback and Iteration:**

   - Gather feedback from stakeholders and users during and after each Sprint to inform future iterations and improvements.

10. Continuous Improvement:

- Conduct regular retrospectives to reflect on team performance and identify opportunities for process improvement.

Best Practices for Implementing Agile in IT Projects:

1. **Start Small:** Begin with a pilot Agile project to gain experience and refine Agile practices before scaling up.

2. **Strong Leadership:** Leadership support is crucial for a successful Agile implementation, as it helps overcome resistance to change.

3. **Clear Roles:** Ensure that Agile roles (Product Owner, Scrum Master, and Development Team) are well-defined, and each member understands their responsibilities.

4. **Continuous Training:** Provide ongoing Agile training to keep team members updated on best practices and methodologies.

5. **Open Communication:** Foster open and transparent communication among team members and stakeholders to maintain alignment and shared understanding.

Challenges in Implementing Agile in IT Projects:

1. **Resistance to Change:** Team members and stakeholders may resist the shift from traditional methodologies to Agile practices.

2. **Cultural Barriers:** Organizational culture and norms may hinder Agile adoption and collaboration.

3. **Estimation and Planning:** Accurate estimation and planning in Agile can be challenging, especially for new teams.

4. **Resource Allocation:** Balancing resources between Agile projects and other ongoing work can be complex.

5. **Scaling Agile:** Transitioning from a small Agile pilot to enterprise-wide adoption can present scaling challenges.

In conclusion, implementing Agile methodologies in IT projects offers a transformative approach to project management, enabling teams to deliver value more efficiently and adapt to change effectively. By following best practices, addressing challenges, and fostering a culture of collaboration and continuous improvement, organizations can successfully embrace Agile principles and reap the benefits of more customer-focused, high-quality, and adaptable IT projects.

CHAPTER 9

Waterfall vs. Agile: Choosing the Right Approach

In the realm of project management, the choice between the Waterfall and Agile methodologies is a pivotal decision that can profoundly impact the success of a project. Waterfall represents a traditional, linear approach, while Agile embodies adaptability and collaboration. Each approach has its strengths and weaknesses, making the selection process a critical factor in project planning. In this introductory exploration, we will navigate the contrasting landscapes of Waterfall and Agile, helping you understand the key differences, considerations, and factors to guide you in choosing the right approach for your specific project requirements.

A. Waterfall Methodology: A Sequential Approach to Project Management

The Waterfall methodology is a traditional and linear project management approach that has been used for decades across various industries. It's characterized by a sequential, phased structure where each phase must be completed before moving on to the next. While Waterfall has its merits, it also has limitations that have led many organizations to explore more flexible approaches like Agile. In this in-depth exploration, we will delve into the Waterfall methodology, examining its principles, phases, advantages, disadvantages, and scenarios where it is best suited.

Principles of the Waterfall Methodology:

1. **Sequential Phases:** Waterfall divides the project into distinct phases, such as requirements, design, implementation, testing, deployment, and maintenance. Each phase must be completed before the next one begins.

2. **Detailed Planning:** The Waterfall approach emphasizes thorough upfront planning, where project requirements and objectives are documented comprehensively at the beginning of the project.

3. **Minimal Customer Involvement:** Customer involvement is typically limited to the initial requirements gathering phase, with less interaction throughout the project.

4. **Documentation:** Extensive documentation is generated at each phase, serving as a record of project progress and specifications.

Phases of the Waterfall Methodology:

1. **Requirements:** Gather and document project requirements, including functionality, features, and constraints.

2. **Design:** Create detailed system and software designs based on the requirements.

3. **Implementation:** Develop the system or software based on the approved design.

4. **Testing:** Conduct comprehensive testing, including unit testing, integration testing, and system testing, to ensure that the product meets requirements.

5. **Deployment:** Deploy the final product or system to the production environment.

6. **Maintenance:** Provide ongoing maintenance and support for the product, addressing any issues or updates as needed.

Advantages of the Waterfall Methodology:

1. **Clarity:** Detailed planning and documentation provide a clear roadmap for the project.

2. **Stability:** Once a phase is completed, it is considered stable and doesn't undergo significant changes.

3. **Predictability:** Waterfall can be predictable in terms of timelines and costs when requirements are well-defined.

4. **Regulated Environments:** It is often favored in highly regulated industries where strict documentation and compliance are required.

Disadvantages of the Waterfall Methodology:

1. **Limited Adaptability:** Waterfall is less adaptable to changing requirements, making it challenging to accommodate evolving customer needs or market conditions.

2. **Customer Disconnect:** Limited customer involvement can result in misunderstandings and a final product that may not fully meet customer expectations.

3. **Longer Time to Delivery:** Projects may take longer to complete due to the sequential nature of the methodology.

4. **Risks Late Discovery:** Issues or defects may only be discovered in later stages, leading to costly rework.

5. **Higher Stress on Documentation:** Extensive documentation can be time-consuming and divert resources from actual development.

Scenarios Where Waterfall Is Suited:

1. **Well-Defined Requirements:** When project requirements are stable, well-understood, and unlikely to change significantly.

2. **Regulated Industries:** In sectors like healthcare and finance, where compliance and documentation are critical.

3. **Small Projects:** For small projects with straightforward objectives and minimal complexity.

4. **Historical Success:** When an organization has a proven track record of success with the Waterfall approach.

In conclusion, the Waterfall methodology offers a structured and systematic approach to project management that can be effective in certain scenarios, especially when requirements are well-defined and change is unlikely. However, it may not be the best fit for projects where adaptability, customer collaboration, and quick response to change are paramount. Ultimately, the choice between Waterfall and more flexible methodologies like Agile depends on the specific needs and dynamics of the project and the organization's culture and goals.

B. Agile Methodology: A Dynamic Approach to Project Management

The Agile methodology is a flexible and iterative approach to project management that has gained widespread adoption in various industries, particularly in software development. It stands in contrast to traditional, linear methodologies like Waterfall by embracing change, customer collaboration, and adaptive planning. Agile methodologies prioritize delivering incremental value, allowing teams to respond quickly to evolving requirements and market dynamics. In this in-depth exploration, we will delve into the Agile methodology, examining its principles, key frameworks, advantages, disadvantages, and scenarios where it excels.

Principles of the Agile Methodology:

Agile methodologies are guided by a set of principles outlined in the Agile Manifesto:

1. **Individuals and interactions over processes and tools:** Agile values people and their communication over rigid processes and tools.

2. **Working software over comprehensive documentation:** Agile prioritizes delivering a working product incrementally over extensive documentation.

3. **Customer collaboration over contract negotiation:** Agile encourages collaboration with customers and stakeholders to ensure the product aligns with their needs.

4. **Responding to change over following a plan:** Agile embraces change and adapts to evolving requirements rather than strictly adhering to a predefined plan.

Key Agile Frameworks:

Several Agile frameworks have emerged over the years to guide the implementation of Agile principles. Some of the most prominent ones include:

1. **Scrum:** Scrum is a widely adopted Agile framework characterized by short, time-boxed iterations called "Sprints,"

daily stand-up meetings, and well-defined roles such as the Product Owner, Scrum Master, and Development Team.

2. **Kanban:** Kanban is a visual project management approach that focuses on visualizing work, limiting work in progress, and optimizing workflow.

3. **Extreme Programming (XP):** XP is an Agile methodology that emphasizes engineering practices such as test-driven development (TDD), pair programming, and continuous integration.

4. **Lean:** Lean principles aim to reduce waste and improve efficiency, making it a valuable addition to Agile practices.

Advantages of the Agile Methodology:

1. **Adaptability:** Agile is highly adaptable to changing requirements, making it suitable for projects with evolving customer needs or market conditions.

2. **Customer-Centric:** Agile methodologies prioritize customer collaboration and continuous feedback, resulting in products that better meet customer expectations.

3. **Faster Time-to-Market:** Incremental development allows for earlier delivery of valuable product increments, reducing time-to-market.

4. **Higher Quality:** Continuous testing and validation in Agile result in higher-quality software with fewer defects.

5. **Improved Team Collaboration:** Agile practices foster open communication and collaboration among cross-functional teams.

Disadvantages of the Agile Methodology:

1. **Complexity:** Agile can be complex to implement, especially in large organizations or projects.

2. **Lack of Documentation:** Agile's focus on working software may lead to minimal documentation, which can be a challenge in regulated industries.

3. **Customer Availability:** Agile relies on frequent customer involvement, which may not be feasible in all projects.

4. **Resource Allocation:** Balancing resources between Agile projects and other ongoing work can be challenging.

Scenarios Where Agile Excels:

1. **Uncertain Requirements:** When project requirements are expected to evolve or are not fully known at the outset.

2. **Rapid Development:** For projects that require a quick response to changing market conditions or competitive pressures.

3. **Innovative Solutions:** When the goal is to develop innovative products or solutions that benefit from ongoing customer feedback.

4. **Cross-Functional Teams:** In environments where cross-functional collaboration is essential for success.

In conclusion, the Agile methodology offers a dynamic and customer-focused approach to project management that excels in scenarios where change is a constant and customer collaboration is critical. By embracing Agile principles and selecting the most suitable framework for the project's needs, organizations can leverage its adaptability and iterative nature to deliver high-quality products that meet customer expectations and respond effectively to evolving market dynamics.

C. Hybrid Approaches in Project Management: Bridging the Gap Between Agile and Waterfall

Hybrid approaches in project management are gaining prominence as organizations seek to leverage the strengths of both Agile and Waterfall methodologies to address diverse project requirements. These approaches aim to strike a balance between the structured, sequential nature of Waterfall and the flexibility and adaptability of Agile. Hybrid models provide organizations with the agility to manage change while maintaining the discipline of well-defined processes. In this in-depth exploration, we will delve into hybrid approaches, examining their principles, benefits, challenges, and scenarios where they are most effective.

Principles of Hybrid Approaches:

Hybrid approaches integrate elements of both Agile and Waterfall methodologies, allowing organizations to tailor project management practices to their specific needs. The principles of hybrid approaches include:

1. **Flexibility and Adaptability:** Hybrid models embrace change and adaptability while maintaining structured processes.

2. **Progressive Elaboration:** Projects may begin with a well-defined plan but allow for progressive elaboration as more information becomes available.

3. **Phased Delivery:** Projects are divided into phases, with some phases following a traditional Waterfall approach and others adopting Agile practices.

4. **Risk Mitigation:** Hybrid approaches often incorporate risk management techniques to address uncertainties and changes effectively.

Benefits of Hybrid Approaches:

1. **Customization:** Organizations can tailor project management practices to suit specific project requirements, optimizing the balance between structure and flexibility.

2. **Risk Management:** Hybrid models provide mechanisms for identifying and mitigating risks, allowing for early adaptation to changing circumstances.

3. **Stakeholder Engagement:** Hybrid approaches can involve stakeholders more effectively, particularly when Agile practices are used for customer collaboration.

4. **Predictability:** The structured phases of a hybrid approach can provide a degree of predictability in terms of project milestones and deliverables.

Challenges of Hybrid Approaches:

1. **Complexity:** Managing hybrid projects can be complex, requiring a deep understanding of both Agile and Waterfall methodologies.

2. **Resource Allocation:** Balancing resources between different phases or teams following different methodologies can be challenging.

3. **Integration:** Ensuring seamless integration between Agile

and Waterfall phases can be a logistical challenge.

4. **Change Management:** Transitioning to a hybrid approach may require a cultural shift within the organization.

Scenarios Where Hybrid Approaches Are Effective:

1. **Mixed Requirements:** Projects with mixed requirements, where some elements are well-defined and stable (suitable for Waterfall) while others are subject to change (suitable for Agile).

2. **Regulated Industries:** In industries with strict compliance and documentation requirements, where Waterfall may be mandated for certain phases.

3. **Longer-Term Projects:** For projects that span an extended period, where Agile's adaptability can be particularly valuable in later phases.

4. **Complex Projects:** In projects with a high degree of complexity, where the structured approach of Waterfall can help manage risk.

Examples of Hybrid Approaches:

1. **Water-Scrum-Fall:** In this model, the project begins with a Waterfall phase (requirements and planning), followed by iterative development using Scrum, and concludes with

Waterfall for testing and deployment.

2. **Agile with Stage-Gate:** An Agile framework is used for development, but key decision points or gates are incorporated, where the project must align with predefined criteria before proceeding.

3. **Agile-Waterfall Hybrid Teams:** Different project teams within an organization may follow either Agile or Waterfall, with coordination to ensure integration.

In conclusion, hybrid approaches in project management offer organizations the flexibility to adapt to changing requirements while maintaining the structure of traditional methodologies. By carefully selecting and customizing the elements of Agile and Waterfall that best suit their project needs, organizations can harness the benefits of both approaches and improve their ability to deliver successful projects in diverse and dynamic environments.

D. Selecting the Appropriate Methodology: A Critical Decision in Project Management

Selecting the right project management methodology is a crucial decision that can significantly impact a project's success. The choice between Agile, Waterfall, Hybrid, or other specialized methodologies should align with the project's goals, requirements, and organizational context. In this in-depth exploration, we will delve into the factors, considerations, and steps involved in selecting the most appropriate methodology for a given project.

Factors to Consider When Selecting a Methodology:

1. **Project Objectives:** Begin by defining the project's objectives and desired outcomes. Consider whether the project is focused on delivering a well-defined product or if it involves innovation and evolving requirements.

2. **Project Scope and Complexity:** Assess the scope and complexity of the project. Waterfall may be suitable for projects with stable, well-understood requirements, while Agile is better suited for projects with evolving requirements and high uncertainty.

3. **Customer Involvement:** Determine the level of customer involvement required. Agile methodologies prioritize frequent customer collaboration, while Waterfall typically involves less customer interaction.

4. **Regulatory and Compliance Requirements:** Consider any industry-specific regulations or compliance requirements. Some industries, such as healthcare and finance, may necessitate a Waterfall or hybrid approach to meet documentation and auditing needs.

5. **Resource Constraints:** Evaluate resource availability, including the size and skills of the project team, budget constraints, and time limitations. Agile may require a more significant commitment of resources for frequent iterations.

6. **Organizational Culture:** Assess the organization's culture and readiness for change. Some organizations may be more inclined to adopt Agile principles, while others may prefer the structure of Waterfall.

Steps to Selecting the Appropriate Methodology:

1. **Define Project Objectives and Requirements:**

   - Clearly articulate the project's objectives, deliverables, and success criteria.

   - Identify any constraints or limitations, such as budget, timeline, or available resources.

2. **Assess Project Characteristics:**

   - Analyze the project's scope, complexity, and uncertainty regarding requirements.

   - Consider the level of customer engagement required throughout the project.

3. **Review Regulatory Requirements:**

   - If the project operates in a regulated industry, assess the compliance requirements and documentation standards.

4. **Evaluate Organizational Readiness:**

   - Gauge the organization's willingness and capacity to adopt Agile or other methodologies.

   - Consider the level of training and cultural change required.

5. **Engage Stakeholders:**

   - Involve key stakeholders, including project sponsors, customers, and team members, in the decision-making process.

   - Gather input and feedback on the preferred methodology.

6. **Select the Appropriate Methodology:**

   - Based on the factors and assessments, make an informed decision regarding the most suitable methodology.

   - Consider hybrid approaches if project characteristics

suggest a mix of Agile and Waterfall elements.

7. **Create a Methodology Implementation Plan:**

   - Develop a plan that outlines how the chosen methodology will be implemented, including training, roles, processes, and tools.

8. **Iterate and Adapt:**

   - Continuously monitor the project's progress and adapt the methodology as needed. Agile methodologies encourage inspecting and adapting throughout the project.

Common Methodology Selection Scenarios:

1. **Agile for Innovation:** Agile is often chosen for projects that require innovation, flexibility, and a high degree of customer involvement, such as software development for emerging markets.

2. **Waterfall for Stability:** Waterfall is preferred when project requirements are well-defined, and stability and predictability are essential, such as construction projects or manufacturing processes.

3. **Hybrid for Mixed Requirements:** Projects with both stable and evolving requirements may benefit from a hybrid

approach, with Waterfall phases for stable elements and Agile iterations for dynamic components.

4. **Regulated Industries:** Highly regulated industries, like healthcare and finance, often opt for Waterfall or hybrid approaches to meet compliance and documentation requirements.

In conclusion, selecting the appropriate project management methodology is a critical decision that should align with the project's objectives, scope, constraints, and organizational context. It requires a thorough assessment of project characteristics and stakeholder input. By choosing the right methodology and implementing it effectively, organizations can enhance their project management capabilities and increase the likelihood of successful project outcomes.

CHAPTER 10

Managing Remote and Distributed Teams: Navigating the New Landscape of Work

In an increasingly globalized and technology-driven world, the concept of work has undergone a significant transformation. Managing remote and distributed teams has become not only a necessity but also an opportunity for organizations to tap into a diverse talent pool and adapt to changing work dynamics. In this introductory exploration, we will delve into the challenges, strategies, tools, and best practices involved in effectively managing teams that are geographically dispersed. Whether you're a team leader, manager, or part of a remote team, understanding the nuances of remote work management is essential in today's professional landscape.

A. Challenges of Remote Project Management: Overcoming Distance and Dispersal

Remote project management presents unique challenges that require adaptation, technology, and effective leadership to overcome. Managing teams spread across different locations, time zones, and cultures can be complex, but with the right strategies, it's possible to ensure productivity, collaboration, and project success. In this in-depth exploration, we will delve into the key challenges faced by remote project managers and discuss practical solutions to address them.

1. Communication Barriers:

Challenge: Effective communication is often cited as the most significant challenge in remote project management. Communication barriers can arise from differences in time zones, language, and communication tools.

Solution:

- Establish clear communication protocols and expectations.

- Use collaboration and communication tools to bridge geographical gaps.

- Schedule regular video conferences and virtual meetings to facilitate face-to-face communication.

2. Lack of Team Cohesion:

Challenge: Building and maintaining team cohesion can be challenging when team members are geographically dispersed. Team bonding and shared experiences can be limited.

Solution:

- Organize virtual team-building activities and social

interactions.

- Foster a sense of belonging through team identity and common goals.

- Encourage open and transparent communication among team members.

3. Time Zone Differences:

Challenge: Coordinating work across different time zones can lead to delays in communication and decision-making, impacting project timelines.

Solution:

- Establish clear working hours and availability expectations.

- Use tools that facilitate asynchronous communication, such as shared project boards and messaging apps.

- Plan meetings and collaboration sessions at times convenient for all team members.

4. Accountability and Productivity Monitoring:

Challenge: Ensuring that team members remain productive and accountable for their tasks can be challenging without physical oversight.

Solution:

- Define clear project objectives and milestones.

- Implement project management tools to track progress and monitor task completion.

- Set up regular check-ins and status updates to review progress and address any issues.

5. Data Security and Privacy:

Challenge: Remote work may pose security risks, especially when team members access sensitive data from different locations and devices.

Solution:

- Implement robust cybersecurity measures, including secure access protocols and data encryption.

- Provide training to team members on data security best practices.

- Use secure and trusted collaboration tools and platforms.

6. Overcoming Cultural Differences:

Challenge: Managing culturally diverse teams can lead to misunderstandings and conflicts if not handled properly.

Solution:

- Foster cultural awareness and sensitivity among team members.

- Encourage open dialogue and respectful communication.

- Seek cultural training or consulting if needed.

7. Isolation and Burnout:

Challenge: Remote team members may experience isolation and burnout due to the lack of separation between work and personal life.

Solution:

- Promote work-life balance and set clear boundaries.

- Encourage breaks and time away from screens.

- Provide mental health resources and support.

8. Technology Issues:

Challenge: Technical difficulties, such as unreliable internet connections or software glitches, can disrupt work and collaboration.

Solution:

- Ensure team members have access to reliable technology and provide technical support.

- Have backup communication methods in place for when technical issues arise.

- Choose robust and well-maintained collaboration tools.

In conclusion, remote project management is a dynamic field that requires proactive strategies to address its unique challenges. Effective communication, clear expectations, collaboration tools, and a supportive team culture are essential for overcoming these challenges and ensuring that remote projects run smoothly and successfully. By embracing remote work management practices and continuously adapting to evolving circumstances, organizations can harness the benefits of a distributed workforce while minimizing its potential pitfalls.

B. Tools and Technologies for Remote Collaboration: Empowering Virtual Teams

The rise of remote work has been accompanied by a proliferation of tools and technologies designed to facilitate remote collaboration and communication. Whether teams are spread across different locations, time zones, or even continents, these tools enable seamless interactions, efficient project management, and productive teamwork. In this in-depth exploration, we will delve into the essential tools and technologies for remote collaboration, highlighting their features, advantages, and considerations for effective use.

1. Video Conferencing Tools:

Features: Video conferencing tools like Zoom, Microsoft Teams, and Cisco Webex offer real-time audio and video communication, screen sharing, chat, and virtual meeting rooms.

Advantages:

- Face-to-face interactions foster a sense of connection.

- Screen sharing enhances visual communication and presentations.

- Chat and file sharing facilitate real-time collaboration.

Considerations:

- Ensure a stable internet connection for high-quality video and audio.

- Familiarize team members with the features to maximize engagement.

2. Messaging and Chat Apps:

Features: Messaging and chat apps like Slack, Microsoft

Teams, and Discord provide instant messaging, channel-based communication, and file sharing.

Advantages:

- Real-time chat supports quick questions and casual communication.

- Channel organization keeps conversations organized by topic or project.

- Integration with other tools streamlines workflow.

Considerations:

- Set clear guidelines for channel usage and etiquette to avoid information overload.

- Use notifications mindfully to prevent distraction.

3. Project Management Software:

Features: Project management tools such as Asana, Trello, and Jira enable task and project tracking, progress monitoring, and collaboration on project-specific boards.

Advantages:

- Visual project boards provide clarity on tasks and timelines.

- Assigning responsibilities and due dates enhances

accountability.

- Integration with other tools centralizes project information.

Considerations:

- Customize project management tools to fit the team's specific workflow.

- Regularly update task statuses to maintain transparency.

4. Document Collaboration:

Features: Document collaboration tools like Google Workspace (formerly G Suite), Microsoft 365, and Dropbox Paper enable real-time editing, commenting, and version control of documents, spreadsheets, and presentations.

Advantages:

- Simultaneous editing supports collaborative document creation.

- Comments and feedback streamline the review and revision process.

- Version history prevents data loss and allows for easy rollbacks.

Considerations:

- Train team members on collaborative document etiquette to prevent conflicts.

- Implement access controls to safeguard sensitive documents.

5. Virtual Whiteboards:

Features: Virtual whiteboard tools such as Miro and Microsoft Whiteboard offer a digital canvas for brainstorming, mind mapping, and visual collaboration.

Advantages:

- Visual brainstorming enhances creativity and idea sharing.

- Collaborative boards facilitate team workshops and planning sessions.

- Integration with video conferencing tools supports real-time collaboration.

Considerations:

- Ensure everyone has access to the virtual whiteboard tool and knows how to use it effectively.

- Save and share board content for future reference.

6. Cloud Storage and File Sharing:

Features: Cloud storage services like Dropbox, Google Drive, and OneDrive allow teams to store, share, and access files from anywhere with an internet connection.

Advantages:

- Centralized storage ensures data accessibility and backup.

- File sharing links simplify document distribution.

- Collaboration features enable multiple users to work on files simultaneously.

Considerations:

- Implement file organization and naming conventions to maintain order.

- Set access permissions to protect sensitive data.

7. Virtual Private Networks (VPNs):

Features: VPNs like NordVPN and ExpressVPN encrypt internet connections, ensuring security and privacy when accessing corporate networks and data remotely.

Advantages:

- Securely access company resources over untrusted networks.

- Protect data from interception and unauthorized access.

- Maintain compliance with security regulations.

Considerations:

- Choose a reliable VPN service and configure it correctly.

- Train team members on VPN usage and best practices.

8. Webinar and Webinar Hosting Platforms:

Features: Webinar platforms like GoToWebinar and WebEx Events enable organizations to host virtual events, webinars, and online training sessions with large audiences.

Advantages:

- Engage with a broad audience and generate leads or educate participants.

- Interactive features like polls, Q&A, and chat enhance participant engagement.

- Recording and archiving webinars for on-demand access.

Considerations:

- Plan and promote webinars effectively to maximize attendance.

- Ensure technical readiness and rehearsal before the live event.

In conclusion, the tools and technologies for remote collaboration have revolutionized the way teams work together, allowing for flexibility, efficiency, and productivity in remote and distributed work environments. To maximize the benefits of these tools, it's essential to choose the right ones for your team's specific needs, provide adequate training and support, and establish clear communication and collaboration guidelines. With the right technology stack and effective use, remote teams can thrive and achieve their project goals regardless of geographical boundaries.

C. Best Practices for Leading Distributed Teams: Navigating the Challenges of Remote Work

Leading distributed teams, where team members are geographically dispersed, is a skill that has become increasingly vital in the modern workplace. While remote work offers flexibility and access to a global talent pool, it also poses unique challenges related to communication, collaboration, and team cohesion. In this in-depth exploration, we will delve into best practices for effectively leading distributed teams, fostering productivity, engagement, and project success.

1. Establish Clear Communication Protocols:

Practice: Define and communicate clear guidelines for communication, including preferred channels, response times, and the use of asynchronous vs. synchronous communication.

Rationale: Clear communication protocols help prevent misunderstandings and ensure that team members are on the same page despite geographical differences.

2. Leverage Technology for Collaboration:

Practice: Invest in collaboration tools and technologies that enable seamless communication, file sharing, project management, and virtual meetings.

Rationale: The right technology stack can bridge the physical distance between team members and facilitate effective collaboration.

3. Define Roles and Responsibilities:

Practice: Clearly define team roles, responsibilities, and expectations. Assign ownership of tasks and projects to specific team members.

Rationale: Well-defined roles minimize confusion, increase accountability, and ensure that everyone understands their contributions to the team's goals.

4. Establish Regular Check-Ins:

Practice: Schedule regular team meetings, one-on-one check-ins, and project status updates. Consider time zones to accommodate team members' availability.

Rationale: Regular communication fosters a sense of connection, allows for progress tracking, and provides an opportunity to address challenges promptly.

5. Foster Team Bonding:

Practice: Organize virtual team-building activities, social events, and opportunities for informal interactions to strengthen team cohesion.

Rationale: Team bonding activities create a sense of belonging and camaraderie among remote team members.

6. Encourage Transparent Documentation:

Practice: Document project plans, decisions, and key information in shared repositories accessible to all team members.

Rationale: Transparent documentation ensures that team members have access to essential information and can refer back to it as needed.

7. Promote Work-Life Balance:

Practice: Encourage team members to maintain a healthy work-life balance by setting clear boundaries and respecting non-working hours.

Rationale: Burnout can be a significant concern in remote work, and promoting work-life balance helps maintain team members' well-being.

8. Recognize and Celebrate Achievements:

Practice: Acknowledge and celebrate individual and team achievements, milestones, and contributions.

Rationale: Recognition and celebration boost morale, motivation, and a sense of accomplishment among team members.

9. Emphasize Results Over Hours:

Practice: Evaluate team members based on their contributions, results, and the quality of their work rather than the number of hours they put in.

Rationale: Focusing on results fosters a results-oriented culture and allows team members to manage their work on their own schedules.

10. Provide Ongoing Training:

Practice: Offer continuous training and professional development opportunities to keep remote team members updated on industry trends and best practices.

Rationale: Ongoing training ensures that team members remain skilled and adaptable in a rapidly changing work environment.

11. Embrace Cultural Sensitivity:

Practice: Encourage cultural sensitivity and awareness among team members to promote effective cross-cultural collaboration.

Rationale: In a diverse global team, cultural understanding enhances communication and minimizes misunderstandings.

12. Lead by Example:

Practice: As a leader, set a positive example by adhering to guidelines, being responsive, and demonstrating a strong work ethic.

Rationale: Leaders' behavior influences the team's culture and work habits.

13. Address Conflict Swiftly:

Practice: Address conflicts or misunderstandings promptly and privately. Encourage open and respectful dialogue to resolve issues.

Rationale: Resolving conflicts prevents them from escalating and negatively impacting team dynamics.

In conclusion, leading distributed teams effectively requires a combination of clear communication, the right tools and technologies, strong leadership, and a focus on team cohesion. By implementing these best practices, organizations can harness the benefits of remote work while mitigating its challenges, ultimately leading to productive, engaged, and successful distributed teams.

CHAPTER 11

IT Project Management Tools and Software: Empowering Project Success in the Digital Age

In the dynamic landscape of IT project management, the role of tools and software cannot be overstated. As technology evolves, so does the need for robust solutions that streamline project planning, execution, monitoring, and control. IT project management tools and software have become indispensable assets, empowering teams to collaborate efficiently, manage resources effectively, and deliver projects on time and within budget. In this introductory exploration, we will embark on a journey through the world of IT project management tools and software, uncovering their significance, features, and their impact on the success of IT projects in today's digital era.

A. Project Management Software Overview: Streamlining IT Project Success

Project management software is the backbone of modern IT project management, providing the digital infrastructure necessary to plan, execute, monitor, and control projects efficiently. These software solutions offer a wide range of features and tools that empower project managers, teams, and stakeholders to collaborate, stay organized, and achieve project objectives. In this in-depth exploration, we will delve into the essential aspects of project management software, its key features, benefits, and considerations for selecting the right tool for your IT project.

Key Features of Project Management Software:

1. **Task and Project Planning:** Project management software allows users to create detailed project plans, defining tasks, dependencies, timelines, and milestones. This feature ensures that project objectives are well-defined and achievable.

2. **Resource Management:** Efficient allocation of resources, such as team members, equipment, and materials, is critical to project success. Project management tools provide resource management features to optimize resource utilization.

3. **Collaboration and Communication:** Collaboration tools, including messaging, file sharing, and discussion boards, enable team members to communicate and work together seamlessly, even in remote or distributed settings.

4. **Gantt Charts and Timelines:** Gantt charts visually represent project schedules, helping project managers and teams understand task sequences, durations, and critical paths.

5. **Document Management:** Storing and organizing project-related documents, such as specifications, designs, and

reports, is made easy with document management features.

6. **Task Assignment and Tracking:** Project management software allows project managers to assign tasks to team members, track progress, and monitor task completion in real time.

7. **Budgeting and Cost Management:** Effective budgeting and cost estimation are essential for project success. Project management tools provide features for budget creation, expense tracking, and cost control.

8. **Reporting and Analytics:** Robust reporting and analytics features enable project managers to generate insights into project performance, identify bottlenecks, and make data-driven decisions.

9. **Risk Management:** Identifying, assessing, and mitigating risks is crucial in IT project management. Project management software often includes risk management tools to manage uncertainties.

10. **Integration and Compatibility:** Integration capabilities with other software and tools, such as email clients, calendar apps, and third-party applications, enhance the software's usability and versatility.

Benefits of Using Project Management Software:

1. **Improved Efficiency:** Project management software streamlines project workflows, reducing manual administrative tasks and saving time for project teams.

2. **Enhanced Collaboration:** Collaboration tools within the software enable real-time communication and file sharing, fostering collaboration among team members, regardless of their location.

3. **Better Resource Allocation:** Resource management features help project managers optimize resource allocation, ensuring that the right skills are assigned to the right tasks.

4. **Greater Visibility:** Project managers gain greater visibility into project progress, enabling them to make informed decisions and adjustments as needed.

5. **Reduced Errors:** Automation and standardized processes reduce the likelihood of errors and inconsistencies in project planning and execution.

6. **Increased Accountability:** Task assignment and tracking features promote accountability among team members, as responsibilities are clearly defined and monitored.

7. **Scalability:** Project management software can scale to accommodate projects of varying sizes and complexities, from

small IT projects to large enterprise initiatives.

Considerations for Selecting Project Management Software:

1. **Project Requirements:** Assess your project's specific needs, such as task complexity, team size, and communication preferences, to find a tool that aligns with your project's demands.

2. **Scalability:** Choose software that can grow with your project and organization to avoid frequent software migrations.

3. **Ease of Use:** The software should have a user-friendly interface to ensure that team members can quickly adopt and use it effectively.

4. **Cost:** Consider the software's pricing structure, including licensing fees, subscription costs, and any additional charges for advanced features.

5. **Integration:** Ensure that the software integrates seamlessly with other tools and software your team uses.

6. **Customization:** Evaluate the software's customization options to tailor it to your project's unique requirements.

7. **Support and Training:** Check for available customer support, training resources, and user communities to assist

with software implementation and troubleshooting.

In conclusion, project management software is a fundamental tool for IT project success, offering a wide array of features and benefits that enhance collaboration, efficiency, and project control. By carefully assessing project requirements and considering the software's features, scalability, and compatibility, organizations can choose the right project management software to streamline their IT projects and achieve their project goals effectively and efficiently.

B. Selection and Implementation of Project Management Tools: A Strategic Approach

Selecting and implementing the right project management (PM) tools is a crucial step in ensuring the success of any project, including IT projects. These tools provide the digital infrastructure needed to plan, execute, and monitor projects effectively, streamline communication, and enhance collaboration among team members. However, the selection and implementation process can be complex and require careful consideration to align with the organization's needs and project objectives. In this in-depth exploration, we will delve into the key considerations, best practices, and challenges associated with selecting and implementing project management tools.

Selection of Project Management Tools:

1. **Define Project Requirements:** Before selecting a PM tool, it's essential to understand the specific requirements of your project. Consider factors such as project size, complexity, team size, and the need for collaboration, reporting, or integration with other software.

2. **Evaluate Features and Capabilities:** Create a list of required features and capabilities, such as task management, resource allocation, reporting, and communication tools. Assess potential tools against these requirements to identify a good fit.

3. **Consider User Experience:** User-friendliness is crucial. Ensure that the chosen tool is intuitive and aligns with the skill levels and preferences of your team members. Test the tool with a pilot group if possible.

4. **Scalability:** Consider the tool's scalability. Will it accommodate future project growth or changes in the organization's needs? Look for a tool that can adapt as your project portfolio expands.

5. **Integration with Existing Systems:** Assess how well the PM tool integrates with your existing software and tools, such as email, calendars, and document management systems. Seamless integration can enhance efficiency.

6. **Cost and Budget:** Evaluate the total cost of ownership, including licensing fees, subscription costs, training, and implementation expenses. Ensure the tool aligns with your budget constraints.

7. **Customization Options:** Some projects may require specific workflows or features. Consider whether the tool allows for customization to adapt to your project's unique requirements.

8. **User Training and Support:** Investigate the availability of training resources, documentation, customer support, and user communities. Adequate training and support are essential for successful implementation.

Implementation of Project Management Tools:

1. **Clearly Define Objectives:** Establish clear implementation objectives and goals. What do you aim to achieve with the PM tool? Define success criteria to measure progress.

2. **Select Implementation Team:** Form a dedicated team responsible for the tool's implementation, including project managers, administrators, and IT support.

3. **Develop a Implementation Plan:** Create a detailed project plan outlining the timeline, milestones, and tasks associated with the tool's deployment. Ensure that all team members understand their roles and responsibilities.

4. **Data Migration and Setup:** If migrating from existing systems, plan for data migration and ensure that historical project data is preserved and accessible within the new tool.

5. **Training and Onboarding:** Provide comprehensive training for all team members who will use the tool. Offer ongoing support and resources to address questions and challenges.

6. **Change Management:** Implement a change management strategy to prepare your team for the transition. Communicate the benefits of the new tool and address concerns.

7. **Pilot Phase:** Consider running a pilot phase with a small team or select projects to test the tool's functionality and gather feedback for adjustments.

8. **Monitor and Evaluate:** Continuously monitor the implementation process and gather feedback from users. Make adjustments as necessary to optimize tool usage.

Challenges in Selection and Implementation:

1. **Resistance to Change:** Team members may resist adopting new tools, particularly if they are accustomed to existing processes. Effective change management is crucial.

2. **Integration Challenges:** Integrating the new tool with existing systems can be complex, potentially leading to technical challenges and compatibility issues.

3. **Data Migration Issues:** Migrating data from legacy systems may result in data loss or inconsistencies. Thorough planning and testing are necessary.

4. **Training Gaps:** Insufficient training can lead to underutilization of the tool and hinder its effectiveness.

5. **Cost Overruns:** Unexpected costs, such as customization or additional training, can lead to budget overruns if not carefully managed.

In conclusion, the selection and implementation of project management tools require careful planning, evaluation, and execution. By defining project requirements, considering features, and addressing potential challenges, organizations can choose the right tools to support their IT projects effectively. Successful implementation involves a structured approach, clear communication, and ongoing support to ensure that the tool is seamlessly integrated into project workflows, enhancing efficiency and project success.

C. Case Studies of Project Management Tool Usage: Real-World Success Stories

Examining case studies of organizations that have effectively leveraged project management tools provides valuable insights into the impact of these tools on project success. These real-world examples showcase how different industries and companies have harnessed the capabilities of PM tools to streamline processes, improve collaboration, and achieve their project objectives efficiently. In this in-depth exploration, we will explore several case studies that highlight the diverse applications and benefits of project management tools in various contexts.

1. Trello at Buffer: Agile Project Management

Buffer, a social media management company, adopted Trello as its project management tool to embrace agile methodologies and enhance collaboration. Trello's visual boards and cards allowed Buffer's teams to manage tasks, track progress, and maintain transparency. This approach facilitated faster decision-making, adaptability to changing priorities, and improved alignment across distributed teams.

Key Takeaways:

- Visual project management tools can enhance agility and flexibility.

- Transparent task management promotes collaboration and accountability.

2. Asana at Airbnb: Scaling Operations

As Airbnb expanded globally, it faced the challenge of scaling operations efficiently. Airbnb chose Asana as its project management tool to centralize project planning and coordination. Asana enabled Airbnb to streamline cross-functional collaboration, manage work across different time zones, and maintain alignment among various teams and projects.

Key Takeaways:

- Project management tools can support large-scale operations and global expansion.

- Centralized project planning enhances cross-functional collaboration.

3. Jira at NASA's Jet Propulsion Laboratory: Complex Project Management

NASA's Jet Propulsion Laboratory (JPL) manages some of the most complex projects in the world, including missions to Mars. JPL adopted Jira, an issue tracking and project management tool, to manage and coordinate these intricate projects. Jira's capabilities, including task tracking, workflow automation, and reporting, have played a vital role in ensuring the success of JPL's missions.

Key Takeaways:

- Specialized project management tools can address complex project requirements.

- Workflow automation improves efficiency in project management.

4. Smartsheet at Cisco: Cross-Functional Collaboration

Cisco, a global technology leader, utilized Smartsheet as its project management tool to foster cross-functional collaboration. Smartsheet's spreadsheet-like interface and project automation features allowed Cisco's teams to plan and execute projects collaboratively. The tool's flexibility enabled customization to suit various project needs across the organization.

Key Takeaways:

- Customizable project management tools can adapt to diverse project requirements.

- Cross-functional collaboration tools enhance alignment and efficiency.

5. Microsoft Project at Volkswagen: Project Portfolio Management

Volkswagen, one of the world's largest automakers, employed Microsoft Project for project portfolio management. The tool helped Volkswagen prioritize projects, allocate resources effectively, and optimize project portfolios. With Microsoft Project, Volkswagen gained visibility into project progress, resource utilization, and costs, allowing for informed decision-making.

Key Takeaways:

- Project portfolio management tools enable strategic decision-making.

- Resource allocation optimization is critical for large organizations.

6. Wrike at Hootsuite: Remote Team Collaboration

Hootsuite, a social media management platform, adopted Wrike as its project management tool to facilitate remote team collaboration. Wrike's features, such as task management, document sharing, and real-time updates, supported Hootsuite's geographically dispersed teams. This approach improved communication, coordination, and project tracking.

Key Takeaways:

- Project management tools can bridge geographical boundaries in remote work.

- Real-time collaboration features enhance communication.

These case studies illustrate the versatility and impact of project management tools across different industries and organizations. Whether supporting agile methodologies, scaling operations, managing complex projects, fostering cross-functional collaboration, enabling project portfolio management, or facilitating remote team collaboration, these tools have played a pivotal role in enhancing efficiency and project success. By tailoring the tool selection to their specific needs and objectives, organizations can achieve similar benefits and drive their projects to successful outcomes.

CHAPTER 12

IT Governance and Compliance: Navigating the Intersection of Technology and Regulation

In today's digital age, where technology is integral to business operations, IT governance and compliance have emerged as essential components of organizational strategy. These disciplines address the critical need to align technology initiatives with business goals while ensuring adherence to regulatory requirements and industry standards. In this introductory exploration, we will delve into the multifaceted realm of IT governance and compliance, highlighting their significance, principles, and the complex landscape they navigate at the intersection of technology, security, and regulation.

A. Aligning Projects with IT Governance Frameworks: Ensuring Strategic Alignment and Compliance

IT governance is a critical component of an organization's overall governance structure, aiming to ensure that IT investments and initiatives support strategic objectives while maintaining compliance with regulatory requirements and industry standards. To achieve this, organizations often leverage IT governance frameworks. In this in-depth exploration, we will delve into the importance of aligning projects with IT governance frameworks, the key frameworks commonly used, and best practices for ensuring that projects are executed in a manner that aligns with governance principles.

Importance of Aligning Projects with IT Governance Frameworks:

1. **Strategic Alignment:** IT governance frameworks provide a structured approach to aligning IT projects and initiatives with the organization's strategic goals. This alignment ensures that technology investments contribute directly to achieving business objectives.

2. **Risk Mitigation:** Governance frameworks establish controls and processes to mitigate IT-related risks, such as cybersecurity threats, data breaches, and compliance violations. By aligning projects with these frameworks, organizations reduce the likelihood of adverse events.

3. **Efficient Resource Allocation:** Governance frameworks help organizations allocate IT resources efficiently, ensuring that projects receive the necessary funding, personnel, and technology support. This prevents resource wastage and promotes project success.

4. **Compliance Assurance:** Many industries are subject to

regulatory requirements, such as GDPR, HIPAA, or ISO standards. Aligning projects with IT governance frameworks ensures that projects comply with these regulations, reducing legal and financial risks.

Common IT Governance Frameworks:

1. **COBIT (Control Objectives for Information and Related Technologies):** COBIT is a widely recognized framework that focuses on aligning IT activities with business objectives, ensuring effective risk management, and optimizing resource allocation. It provides detailed controls and processes for IT governance.

2. **ITIL (Information Technology Infrastructure Library):** ITIL is a framework that emphasizes service management and delivery. It provides guidelines for managing IT services throughout their lifecycle, ensuring that services meet business needs and are cost-effective.

3. **ISO 27001:** ISO 27001 is an international standard for information security management systems (ISMS). It focuses on protecting sensitive information and managing security risks. Aligning IT projects with ISO 27001 helps ensure data security and compliance.

4. **NIST Cybersecurity Framework:** Developed by the National Institute of Standards and Technology (NIST), this

framework provides guidelines for improving cybersecurity risk management. It includes functions like Identify, Protect, Detect, Respond, and Recover to enhance cybersecurity posture.

5. **TOGAF (The Open Group Architecture Framework):** TOGAF is an enterprise architecture methodology and framework used for developing and managing enterprise architecture. It helps organizations align IT projects with overall business architecture.

Best Practices for Aligning Projects with IT Governance Frameworks:

1. **Define Clear Objectives:** Ensure that each IT project has well-defined objectives that align with the organization's strategic goals and priorities.

2. **Select the Appropriate Framework:** Choose the IT governance framework that best suits your organization's industry, size, and specific needs. Tailor the framework to fit your project's requirements.

3. **Involve Stakeholders:** Engage key stakeholders, including executives, project managers, and IT teams, in the governance process. Collaboration ensures that everyone understands and supports governance principles.

4. **Risk Assessment:** Conduct a thorough risk assessment for each project to identify potential risks and vulnerabilities. Mitigate these risks in line with the governance framework's recommendations.

5. **Document Compliance:** Maintain detailed documentation to demonstrate compliance with the chosen governance framework. This documentation includes policies, procedures, risk assessments, and audit reports.

6. **Regular Auditing and Review:** Continuously monitor projects for compliance and effectiveness. Regular audits and reviews ensure that projects stay aligned with governance principles and can adapt to changing circumstances.

7. **Training and Awareness:** Provide training and awareness programs to educate project teams and stakeholders about the governance framework and its importance.

8. **Communication:** Foster open communication channels between project teams and governance bodies to facilitate information sharing and issue resolution.

In conclusion, aligning IT projects with IT governance frameworks is essential for organizations aiming to maximize the value of their technology investments while minimizing risks. These frameworks provide a structured approach to strategic alignment, risk management, and compliance assurance. By selecting the right framework, involving stakeholders, and following best practices, organizations can ensure that their projects contribute to business success while maintaining governance and compliance standards.

B. Regulatory Compliance in IT Projects: Navigating the Complex Landscape

Regulatory compliance in IT projects is a critical consideration, especially in industries subject to various legal, industry-specific, or regional regulations. It encompasses adherence to laws, standards, and guidelines relevant to data privacy, security, quality, and ethical practices. Ensuring compliance is essential not only for avoiding legal consequences but also for maintaining trust with customers and stakeholders. In this in-depth exploration, we will delve into the multifaceted realm of regulatory compliance in IT projects, including its importance, key regulations, challenges, and best practices for implementation.

Importance of Regulatory Compliance in IT Projects:

1. **Legal Obligation:** Compliance with laws and regulations is a legal requirement in many industries. Failure to comply can result in fines, legal action, and reputational damage.

2. **Data Protection:** Regulations like GDPR (General Data Protection Regulation) and HIPAA (Health Insurance

Portability and Accountability Act) require organizations to protect sensitive data. Compliance safeguards data privacy and security.

3. **Customer Trust:** Demonstrating compliance fosters trust among customers, partners, and stakeholders, as they know their data and interests are protected.

4. **Risk Mitigation:** Compliance helps organizations identify and mitigate potential risks, such as cybersecurity threats and data breaches, reducing the likelihood of adverse events.

Key Regulatory Frameworks and Considerations:

1. **GDPR (General Data Protection Regulation):** GDPR imposes strict rules on data protection and privacy for individuals within the European Union (EU). IT projects involving personal data must comply with GDPR, ensuring transparency, consent, and data subject rights.

2. **HIPAA (Health Insurance Portability and Accountability Act):** HIPAA applies to healthcare organizations in the United States. IT projects in healthcare must comply with HIPAA to protect patient data and maintain confidentiality.

3. **PCI DSS (Payment Card Industry Data Security Standard):** Organizations handling payment card data must adhere to PCI DSS to secure cardholder information.

Compliance ensures the secure processing of financial transactions.

4. **ISO Standards:** Various ISO standards, such as ISO 27001 (information security) and ISO 9001 (quality management), provide guidelines for IT projects to achieve and demonstrate compliance with specific criteria.

5. **Sarbanes-Oxley Act (SOX):** SOX applies to publicly traded companies in the United States and mandates strict financial reporting and internal controls. IT projects related to financial reporting must align with SOX requirements.

Challenges in Achieving Regulatory Compliance:

1. **Complexity of Regulations:** Regulations are often complex, with numerous requirements that can be challenging to interpret and implement.

2. **Rapidly Changing Landscape:** The regulatory landscape evolves, and new laws and amendments are enacted. Staying up-to-date with changes is demanding.

3. **Data Management:** Ensuring the security and privacy of data, especially in IT projects involving vast amounts of data, can be complex and resource-intensive.

4. **Resource Constraints:** Compliance efforts require time, expertise, and resources, which can strain project budgets and

timelines.

5. **Cross-Border Operations:** International organizations face the complexity of complying with regulations in multiple jurisdictions, each with its own requirements.

Best Practices for Achieving Regulatory Compliance:

1. **Understand Applicable Regulations:** Gain a deep understanding of the regulations relevant to your industry and region, seeking legal counsel or compliance experts if necessary.

2. **Risk Assessment:** Conduct thorough risk assessments to identify potential compliance risks in IT projects and prioritize mitigation efforts.

3. **Documentation:** Maintain detailed records of compliance efforts, including policies, procedures, risk assessments, and audit reports.

4. **Education and Training:** Train project teams and staff on compliance requirements, ensuring that they understand their roles and responsibilities.

5. **Continuous Monitoring:** Regularly monitor and audit IT projects to ensure ongoing compliance and quickly address any deviations.

6. **Data Encryption and Security:** Implement robust data encryption and security measures to protect sensitive information.

7. **Vendor Assessment:** Assess the compliance status of third-party vendors and service providers to ensure their practices align with your organization's requirements.

8. **Compliance Software:** Consider using compliance management software to streamline documentation, reporting, and auditing processes.

In conclusion, regulatory compliance in IT projects is a multifaceted endeavor, requiring careful consideration, planning, and implementation. Organizations must navigate a complex landscape of regulations, stay informed about changes, and allocate resources effectively. By adopting best practices and a proactive approach, organizations can not only achieve compliance but also gain a competitive advantage by demonstrating a commitment to data protection, security, and ethical practices.

CHAPTER 13

Project Portfolio Management (PPM): Strategic Excellence in Project Selection and Execution

In the dynamic world of project management, where organizations continually seek to innovate and adapt, Project Portfolio Management (PPM) emerges as a strategic powerhouse. PPM is a disciplined approach that empowers organizations to make informed decisions about which projects to pursue and how to execute them effectively. It involves the careful evaluation, selection, prioritization, and management of a portfolio of projects to align with an organization's overarching goals and objectives. In this introductory exploration, we will delve into the realm of Project Portfolio Management, unveiling its significance, principles, and its role in shaping the strategic direction of modern enterprises.

A. Principles of Project Portfolio Management: Guiding Strategic Excellence

Project Portfolio Management (PPM) is a discipline that empowers organizations to optimize their project portfolios by aligning them with strategic objectives, resource constraints, and risk tolerance. PPM enables organizations to make informed decisions about which projects to undertake, how to prioritize them, and how to ensure successful execution. To effectively implement PPM, organizations adhere to a set of principles that guide their strategic excellence. In this in-depth exploration, we will delve into the core principles of Project Portfolio Management.

1. Alignment with Strategic Objectives:

- **Principle:** All projects within the portfolio must align with the organization's strategic goals and objectives.

- **Rationale:** Aligning projects with the strategic direction ensures that resources and efforts are directed toward initiatives that contribute to the organization's long-term success.

- **Implementation:** Regularly assess project proposals and ongoing projects to ensure they align with strategic objectives. Reject or deprioritize projects that do not align.

2. Prioritization Based on Value:

- **Principle:** Projects should be prioritized based on their potential value to the organization.

- **Rationale:** Prioritization ensures that high-value projects receive adequate attention and resources, maximizing the return on investment.

- **Implementation:** Use objective criteria, such as expected ROI, strategic fit, and market demand, to prioritize projects within the portfolio.

3. Resource Optimization:

- **Principle:** Allocate resources (human, financial, and technological) judiciously to balance project demands and constraints.

- **Rationale:** Resource optimization prevents overcommitment, resource bottlenecks, and project failures due to resource shortages.

- **Implementation:** Regularly assess resource availability and capacity. Adjust project schedules or resource allocation as needed to optimize resource utilization.

4. Risk Management:

- **Principle:** Consider and manage the risks associated with each project within the portfolio.

- **Rationale:** Identifying and mitigating risks ensures that projects are executed with a higher probability of success.

- **Implementation:** Develop risk assessments and mitigation plans for each project. Continuously monitor and update risk assessments throughout project lifecycles.

5. Regular Review and Monitoring:

- **Principle:** Continuously review and monitor the performance and status of projects in the portfolio.

- **Rationale:** Regular reviews provide insights into project progress, enabling timely adjustments and decision-making.

- **Implementation:** Establish a governance structure for regular portfolio reviews. Use key performance indicators (KPIs) to measure project performance.

6. Flexibility and Adaptation:

- **Principle:** Be adaptable and open to adjusting the portfolio as circumstances change.

- **Rationale:** Business environments evolve, and organizations must be prepared to reallocate resources, change priorities, or terminate projects as needed.

- **Implementation:** Develop contingency plans and a process for making changes to the portfolio. Continuously assess the portfolio's alignment with organizational goals.

7. Transparency and Communication:

- **Principle:** Maintain transparency in decision-making and communicate portfolio status and decisions to stakeholders.

- **Rationale:** Transparency fosters trust among stakeholders and ensures that decisions are based on objective criteria.

- **Implementation:** Establish clear communication channels for portfolio updates and decision-making. Involve key stakeholders in portfolio governance.

8. Continuous Improvement:

- **Principle:** Promote a culture of continuous improvement within the PPM process.

- **Rationale:** Continuous improvement ensures that the PPM process remains effective and responsive to changing business conditions.

- **Implementation:** Encourage feedback from project teams and stakeholders. Use lessons learned from completed projects to refine the PPM process.

By adhering to these core principles of Project Portfolio Management, organizations can effectively navigate the complexities of managing a portfolio of projects. PPM provides a structured approach to strategic decision-making, resource allocation, and risk management, enabling organizations to achieve their goals while maximizing the value of their project investments.

B. Maximizing Project Impact through Project Portfolio Management (PPM): A Strategic Imperative

Project Portfolio Management (PPM) is not merely a process for selecting and managing projects; it's a strategic imperative for organizations seeking to optimize resources, align project outcomes with business objectives, and maximize the impact of their project investments. In this in-depth exploration, we will delve into how PPM serves as a catalyst for maximizing project impact, ensuring that organizations achieve their strategic goals efficiently and effectively.

1. Prioritizing the Right Projects:

- **Strategic Project Selection:** PPM enables organizations to select projects that align with their strategic goals. By evaluating project proposals based on factors such as strategic fit, expected ROI, and market demand, PPM ensures that projects with the highest potential for impact are given priority.

- **Resource Allocation:** PPM helps organizations allocate resources to projects strategically. High-impact projects receive the necessary resources, ensuring that they can be executed effectively and deliver the expected outcomes.

2. Resource Optimization:

- **Balancing Resources:** PPM helps organizations balance resource constraints by avoiding overallocation or underutilization. Resource optimization ensures that projects have the right mix of human, financial, and technological resources to succeed.

- **Resource Reallocation:** When projects face unforeseen challenges or changing business conditions, PPM provides the flexibility to reallocate resources to maximize impact. Projects with greater potential for impact can receive additional resources when needed.

3. Risk Management and Mitigation:

- **Risk Assessment:** PPM incorporates risk management into project selection and execution. Projects are evaluated for potential risks, and mitigation plans are developed to address them. This proactive approach minimizes the likelihood of project setbacks.

- **Continuous Monitoring:** Throughout project lifecycles, PPM involves continuous risk monitoring and adjustment of mitigation strategies. This ensures that risks are managed effectively, and projects stay on course to maximize impact.

4. Alignment with Organizational Goals:

- **Strategic Alignment:** PPM ensures that projects are consistently aligned with the organization's strategic objectives. This alignment ensures that project outcomes contribute directly to the organization's long-term success.

- **Regular Review:** PPM involves regular portfolio reviews to assess project alignment. Projects that no longer align with organizational goals can be deprioritized or terminated, freeing up resources for more impactful initiatives.

5. Decision-Making Transparency:

- **Objective Criteria:** PPM relies on objective criteria for project selection and prioritization. This transparency ensures that projects are chosen based on their potential for impact rather than subjective preferences.

- **Stakeholder Involvement:** PPM involves key stakeholders in the decision-making process. Their input and feedback contribute to more informed decisions that align with organizational goals and maximize impact.

6. Continuous Improvement:

- **Feedback Loop:** PPM fosters a culture of continuous improvement. Lessons learned from completed projects are integrated into the PPM process, allowing organizations to refine their approach and make better decisions in the future.

- **Process Refinement:** Organizations use feedback and data from PPM to refine their project selection, resource allocation, and risk management processes continually. This iterative approach enhances the organization's ability to maximize impact.

7. Adaptability to Change:

- **Responsive Decision-Making:** PPM enables organizations to respond quickly to changing business conditions or market dynamics. Projects can be adjusted or reprioritized to seize new opportunities or address emerging challenges.

- **Agility:** PPM supports organizational agility by ensuring that resources can be reallocated to high-impact projects as needed. This adaptability enhances the organization's ability to navigate uncertainty and maximize impact.

In conclusion, Project Portfolio Management (PPM) is a strategic approach that organizations leverage to maximize the impact of their project investments. By aligning projects with strategic goals, optimizing resources, managing risks, and fostering a culture of continuous improvement, PPM empowers organizations to make informed decisions that drive success. It enables organizations to not only deliver projects on time and within budget but also to ensure that these projects contribute significantly to the achievement of overarching business objectives.

CHAPTER 14

Project Management Office (PMO): Orchestrating Project Excellence

In the realm of project management, where the orchestration of multiple initiatives is paramount, the Project Management Office (PMO) emerges as the conductor of organizational success. A PMO is a centralized entity within an organization responsible for defining and maintaining project management standards, processes, and governance. It plays a pivotal role in ensuring that projects are executed efficiently, consistently, and in alignment with strategic objectives. In this introductory exploration, we will delve into the realm of PMO, unveiling its significance, functions, and the pivotal role it plays in driving project excellence within modern enterprises.

A. Role and Functions of a Project Management Office (PMO): The Catalyst for Project Excellence

A Project Management Office (PMO) serves as a strategic driver within organizations, ensuring that projects are executed efficiently, consistently, and in alignment with the organization's strategic objectives. The role and functions of a PMO are multifaceted, encompassing a wide range of responsibilities that contribute to project excellence and organizational success. In this in-depth exploration, we will delve into the core role and functions of a PMO, shedding light on how it supports project management maturity and enhances overall business performance.

1. Strategic Alignment:

- **Role:** The PMO aligns project portfolios with the organization's strategic objectives. It ensures that projects are selected and executed in a manner that directly contributes to the organization's long-term goals.

- **Functions:**

  - Collaborating with senior management to define strategic objectives.

  - Evaluating project proposals for strategic alignment.

  - Prioritizing projects based on their strategic significance.

  - Monitoring project progress to ensure continued alignment.

2. Governance and Standards:

- **Role:** The PMO establishes project management standards, processes, and best practices to create a consistent and standardized approach to project execution.

- **Functions:**

  - Developing project management methodologies and frameworks.

  - Defining project management templates and documentation standards.

  - Conducting project management training and certification programs.

  - Enforcing project governance and compliance.

3. Portfolio Management:

- **Role:** The PMO oversees the entire project portfolio, ensuring that resources are allocated appropriately, and projects are executed efficiently.

- **Functions:**

  - Assessing project feasibility and resource requirements.

  - Balancing resource allocation across projects.

  - Regularly reviewing project status and performance.

  - Recommending adjustments to project priorities.

4. Risk Management:

- **Role:** The PMO identifies, assesses, and manages risks across projects to minimize their impact on project success.

- **Functions:**

  - Conducting risk assessments for each project.

  - Developing risk mitigation plans.

  - Monitoring and communicating risk status.

  - Implementing risk management best practices.

5. Quality Assurance:

- **Role:** The PMO ensures that project deliverables meet the organization's quality standards and that projects are executed according to best practices.

- **Functions:**

  - Establishing quality assurance processes and standards.

  - Conducting project audits and reviews.

  - Implementing continuous improvement initiatives.

  - Providing project teams with quality management

guidance.

6. Resource Management:

- **Role:** The PMO manages and optimizes the allocation of resources, including human, financial, and technological, to support project success.

- **Functions:**

  - Tracking resource availability and demand.

  - Allocating resources based on project priorities.

  - Resolving resource conflicts.

  - Identifying opportunities for resource optimization.

7. Reporting and Communication:

- **Role:** The PMO facilitates transparent communication by providing project stakeholders with accurate and timely information on project status and performance.

- **Functions:**

  - Developing standardized project reporting templates.

  - Generating regular project status reports.

  - Facilitating communication between project teams and

stakeholders.

- Ensuring that project issues and risks are appropriately communicated.

8. Knowledge Management:

- **Role:** The PMO captures and disseminates knowledge and best practices gained from past projects to improve future project performance.

- **Functions:**

    - Creating a knowledge repository for project documentation.

    - Conducting lessons learned sessions after project completion.

    - Promoting knowledge sharing among project teams.

    - Providing access to project templates and historical data.

9. Change Management:

- **Role:** The PMO supports organizational change by helping project teams and stakeholders adapt to new processes, technologies, or methodologies.

- **Functions:**

    - Developing change management strategies and plans.

    - Providing change management training and support.

    - Monitoring the adoption of new processes and technologies.

    - Addressing resistance to change and mitigating its impact.

In summary, the PMO plays a central role in orchestrating project excellence within organizations. Its functions span across strategic alignment, governance, portfolio management, risk management, quality assurance, resource management, reporting, knowledge management, and change management. By fulfilling these functions effectively, the PMO not only enhances the success of individual projects but also contributes to the overall performance and success of the organization. It serves as a catalyst for project management maturity and organizational excellence.

B. PMO's Contribution to Project Success: A Strategic Enabler

A Project Management Office (PMO) serves as a strategic enabler within organizations, playing a pivotal role in ensuring the success of individual projects and contributing to the overall achievement of organizational objectives. Its influence extends far beyond administrative support, as it adds value by providing governance, guidance, and resources to optimize project management processes. In this in-depth exploration, we will delve into the significant contributions of a PMO to project success and how it enhances project management maturity.

1. Standardization of Processes and Methodologies:

- **Contribution:** The PMO establishes standardized project management processes, methodologies, and best practices.

- **Impact on Success:** Standardization ensures that project teams follow consistent and proven approaches, reducing the likelihood of errors, missteps, and deviations from best practices. This enhances project success by improving project planning, execution, and delivery.

2. Improved Governance and Accountability:

- **Contribution:** The PMO provides governance structures and enforces project governance policies.

- **Impact on Success:** Governance ensures that projects are executed with transparency, accountability, and compliance. Clear roles and responsibilities lead to better decision-making, risk management, and adherence to project objectives.

3. Resource Allocation and Management:

- **Contribution:** The PMO oversees resource allocation, ensuring that projects have access to the necessary human, financial, and technological resources.

- **Impact on Success:** Proper resource management prevents resource shortages or overcommitment, minimizing disruptions and project delays. Projects can proceed efficiently and meet deadlines.

4. Risk Management and Mitigation:

- **Contribution:** The PMO identifies, assesses, and manages risks across projects.

- **Impact on Success:** Effective risk management reduces the likelihood of project setbacks or failures. Timely identification and mitigation of risks ensure that projects stay on track and within budget.

5. Quality Assurance and Continuous Improvement:

- **Contribution:** The PMO establishes quality assurance processes and encourages continuous improvement.

- **Impact on Success:** Quality assurance ensures that project deliverables meet the organization's standards and expectations. Lessons learned from previous projects lead to process enhancements, reducing errors and enhancing project outcomes.

6. Reporting and Communication:

- **Contribution:** The PMO facilitates transparent communication by providing regular project status reports and updates.

- **Impact on Success:** Effective communication ensures that stakeholders are informed about project progress and issues. It allows for timely decision-making and issue resolution, reducing the impact of potential roadblocks on project success.

7. Knowledge Management and Best Practices:

- **Contribution:** The PMO captures and disseminates knowledge and best practices gained from past projects.

- **Impact on Success:** Access to historical project data and best practices guides project teams. Lessons learned and successful strategies from previous projects can be applied to new initiatives, improving project outcomes.

8. Change Management Support:

- **Contribution:** The PMO supports change management efforts when implementing new project management processes or technologies.

- **Impact on Success:** Change management support ensures that project teams and stakeholders adapt to new practices smoothly. Reduced resistance to change leads to smoother project execution and a higher likelihood of achieving project objectives.

9. Portfolio Management and Strategic Alignment:

- **Contribution:** The PMO oversees the entire project portfolio and ensures alignment with organizational goals.

- **Impact on Success:** Strategic alignment ensures that resources are allocated to projects that contribute directly to the organization's objectives. Projects are executed with a clear understanding of their strategic importance, enhancing the likelihood of achieving success.

In conclusion, a PMO's contribution to project success is multifaceted and extends to various aspects of project management. By providing governance, standardization, resource management, risk mitigation, quality assurance, communication support, knowledge management, change management, and strategic alignment, the PMO enhances the effectiveness and efficiency of project execution. Its role as a strategic enabler ensures that individual projects contribute to the overall success and growth of the organization, making it a critical component of project management maturity within modern enterprises.

CHAPTER 15

Change Management in IT Projects: Navigating the Human Element of Technological Transformation

In the ever-evolving landscape of Information Technology (IT), where innovation and adaptation are constant imperatives, successful project implementation often hinges on more than just technology—it requires adeptly managing the human element of change. Change Management in IT Projects is a vital discipline that addresses the challenges and opportunities presented when introducing new technologies, processes, or systems within an organization. In this introductory exploration, we will delve into the realm of Change Management in IT Projects, shedding light on its significance, principles, and how it empowers organizations to navigate the complexities of technological transformation while ensuring the engagement and buy-in of their most valuable asset: their people.

A. Managing Organizational Change in IT Projects: A Strategic Imperative

Organizational change is an intrinsic part of Information Technology (IT) projects. Implementing new technologies, systems, or processes inherently disrupts established routines and workflows, affecting how people work and interact within an organization. Managing organizational change effectively is a strategic imperative in IT projects to ensure successful adoption, minimize resistance, and maximize the benefits of technological transformation. In this in-depth exploration, we will delve into the complexities of managing organizational change within IT projects and uncover best practices for achieving a smooth transition.

1. Understanding the Dynamics of Change:

- **The Change Curve:** Recognize that individuals experience change differently. The Change Curve model illustrates stages such as denial, resistance, exploration, and commitment. Understanding where individuals are in this curve helps tailor change strategies.

- **Psychological Impact:** Change often triggers fear, uncertainty, and resistance. Acknowledge these emotions and provide support and communication to address them.

2. Creating a Compelling Vision:

- **Clear Vision:** Establish a clear and compelling vision for the change. Explain why the change is necessary, what benefits it will bring, and how it aligns with the organization's goals.

- **Leadership Involvement:** Ensure that senior leadership actively supports and communicates the vision. Leaders serve as role models for embracing change.

**3. Effective Communication:

- **Timely and Transparent Communication:** Communicate consistently and transparently about the change. Address questions, concerns, and provide regular updates.

- **Multi-Channel Approach:** Use various communication channels such as town hall meetings, emails, newsletters, and intranet to reach different audiences.

4. Engaging Stakeholders:

- **Inclusivity:** Involve employees and key stakeholders in the change process. Encourage feedback, ideas, and participation to make them feel part of the solution.

- **Change Champions:** Identify and empower change champions within the organization. These are individuals who support the change and can influence their peers positively.

5. Training and Development:

- **Skills Enhancement:** Provide the necessary training and resources for employees to acquire the skills and knowledge required for the change.

- **Continuous Learning:** Promote a culture of continuous learning and adaptability to keep up with evolving technologies.

6. Change Management Plan:

- **Structured Approach:** Develop a change management plan that outlines the change process, milestones, responsibilities, and timelines.

- **Risk Assessment:** Identify potential obstacles and resistance points in advance and develop strategies to mitigate them.

7. Measuring and Celebrating Success:

- **Key Performance Indicators (KPIs):** Define KPIs to track the progress of the change. Measure the impact on productivity, efficiency, customer satisfaction, and other relevant metrics.

- **Celebrating Milestones:** Recognize and celebrate achievements and milestones along the way. Positive reinforcement reinforces the commitment to change.

8. Sustaining Change:

- **Integration:** Ensure that the change becomes ingrained in the organizational culture. Embed new behaviors and processes into daily operations.

- **Continuous Improvement:** Encourage feedback and adapt to evolving circumstances. Change management is an ongoing process, and adjustments may be necessary.

9. Mitigating Resistance:

- **Active Listening:** Listen actively to concerns and objections. Address them with empathy and data-driven explanations.

- **Creating a Supportive Environment:** Foster an environment where employees feel safe to voice their concerns without fear of retribution.

10. Learn from Experience:

- **Post-Implementation Review:** Conduct a comprehensive review after the change is fully implemented. Identify lessons learned and areas for improvement.

- **Knowledge Transfer:** Share insights and best practices from the change management process with future projects.

Managing organizational change within IT projects is not just about technology; it's about people. By understanding the human dynamics, creating a compelling vision, effective communication, stakeholder engagement, and a structured approach, organizations can navigate the complexities of change successfully. Change management is not a one-size-fits-all process; it's a tailored, strategic approach that maximizes the chances of IT project success while ensuring that the organization and its people thrive in the face of technological transformation.

B. Stakeholder Buy-In and Communication in Organizational Change: Keys to Success

In the realm of organizational change, securing stakeholder buy-in and effective communication are two interrelated pillars that significantly impact the success of any transformation initiative. Whether implementing new technologies, altering processes, or shifting the organizational culture, involving stakeholders and keeping them informed and engaged are crucial components of successful change management. In this in-depth exploration, we will delve into the importance of stakeholder buy-in and communication, strategies for achieving them, and their pivotal role in navigating organizational change effectively.

1. Importance of Stakeholder Buy-In:

- **Alignment with Goals:** Stakeholder buy-in ensures that individuals and groups affected by the change are aligned with the organization's goals and objectives.

- **Mitigating Resistance:** Buy-in minimizes resistance to change, as stakeholders are more likely to support what they understand and feel connected to.

- **Commitment to Success:** When stakeholders are committed to the change's success, they actively contribute to its achievement.

2. Strategies for Securing Stakeholder Buy-In:

- **Clear Communication:** Communicate the rationale, benefits, and expected impact of the change clearly and transparently.

- **Involvement:** Involve stakeholders in the decision-making process, especially in shaping the change's scope and approach.

- **Feedback Loop:** Establish channels for feedback and address concerns and objections promptly.

- **Change Champions:** Identify and empower change champions from within the organization who can influence their peers positively.

3. The Role of Effective Communication:

- **Creating Understanding:** Effective communication ensures that stakeholders understand the reasons for change, what the change entails, and how it will affect them.

- **Managing Expectations:** Clear communication manages stakeholders' expectations about the change's impact on their roles, responsibilities, and the organization as a whole.

- **Building Trust:** Transparency and consistent messaging build trust among stakeholders, reinforcing their commitment to the change.

4. Strategies for Effective Communication:

- **Multi-Channel Approach:** Use a variety of communication channels such as emails, town hall meetings, intranet, and newsletters to reach different audiences.

- **Tailored Messages:** Customize messages to address the unique concerns and interests of different stakeholder groups.

- **Two-Way Communication:** Encourage and facilitate two-way communication, allowing stakeholders to express their thoughts, concerns, and questions.

- **Timeliness:** Ensure that communication is timely, providing information when stakeholders need it to make informed decisions.

5. Overcoming Communication Challenges:

- **Language and Jargon:** Avoid technical jargon and use language that is accessible to all stakeholders.

- **Cultural Sensitivity:** Recognize and respect cultural differences that may impact communication styles and preferences.

- **Resistance:** Address resistance to change proactively by communicating the benefits and addressing concerns openly.

6. Continuous Engagement:

- **Ongoing Communication:** Maintain regular communication throughout the change process, providing updates on progress and milestones.

- **Feedback Mechanisms:** Continuously seek feedback from stakeholders to identify emerging concerns and address them promptly.

- **Celebrate Successes:** Acknowledge and celebrate achievements and milestones along the way to maintain motivation and momentum.

7. Agile Adaptation:

- **Flexibility:** Be prepared to adapt communication strategies based on feedback and changing circumstances.

- **Reinforcement:** Repetition and reinforcement of key messages help ensure that the information is retained and acted upon.

8. Measuring Success:

- **KPIs:** Define key performance indicators (KPIs) related to stakeholder buy-in and communication effectiveness. Measure and analyze these metrics to gauge progress.

- **Surveys and Feedback:** Conduct surveys and collect feedback from stakeholders to assess their satisfaction with the communication process.

In conclusion, stakeholder buy-in and effective communication are integral components of successful organizational change. They build the foundation for collaboration, trust, and commitment necessary for navigating change effectively. Organizations that prioritize stakeholder engagement and clear, transparent communication are better positioned to achieve their change management goals and realize the benefits of transformation initiatives.

CHAPTER 16

Agile Scaling Frameworks: Navigating the Complexities of Large-Scale Agile Adoption

In the ever-evolving landscape of software development and project management, Agile methodologies have proven their worth in delivering flexibility, customer-centricity, and adaptability. However, as organizations grow and undertake increasingly complex projects, the need arises to scale Agile principles and practices to suit larger teams and more extensive endeavors. Agile Scaling Frameworks, a collection of structured approaches and methodologies, have emerged as a response to this challenge. In this introductory exploration, we will delve into the world of Agile Scaling Frameworks, uncovering their significance, principles, and how they empower organizations to extend the benefits of Agile across the enterprise while effectively managing complexity and scale.

A. SAFe (Scaled Agile Framework): Scaling Agile for Enterprise Success

The Scaled Agile Framework (SAFe) is a comprehensive and customizable framework designed to help organizations scale Agile principles and practices across the enterprise. It provides a structured approach to agile transformation, enabling organizations to effectively manage large-scale software development and project initiatives while fostering collaboration, innovation, and continuous delivery. In this in-depth exploration, we will delve into the SAFe framework, its key principles, components, and how it empowers organizations to navigate the complexities of enterprise-level agile adoption.

Key Principles of SAFe:

1. **Lean-Agile Mindset:** SAFe is built upon a Lean-Agile mindset, emphasizing a culture of continuous improvement, customer-centricity, and collaboration. It encourages organizations to embrace the agile values and principles outlined in the Agile Manifesto.

2. **Value Delivery:** SAFe places a strong emphasis on delivering value to customers and end-users. It aligns all activities and decisions with the goal of maximizing value creation.

3. **Organizing Around Value:** SAFe introduces the concept of "Value Streams," which are sequences of steps that deliver value to the customer. It encourages organizations to organize their teams and activities around these value streams.

Key Components of SAFe:

1. **Lean Portfolio Management:** At the highest level, SAFe

introduces Lean Portfolio Management to align strategy and execution by applying lean and systems thinking approaches. This component ensures that the organization is investing in the right initiatives and prioritizing work effectively.

2. **Agile Release Trains (ARTs):** ARTs are teams of Agile teams (typically 5-12 teams) that work together to deliver value. They have a defined mission, a fixed schedule (e.g., 8-12 weeks), and a backlog of prioritized work items.

3. **Program Increment (PI):** The PI is the heartbeat of SAFe. It's a time-boxed planning interval during which an Agile Release Train delivers value in the form of working, tested software and systems.

4. **Team and Technical Agility:** SAFe provides guidance on Agile teams' structure, roles, and responsibilities. It emphasizes technical practices like continuous integration, test automation, and DevOps to ensure teams can deliver high-quality solutions.

5. **Release on Demand:** This aspect of SAFe allows organizations to release value to customers when it's needed. It emphasizes continuous delivery and shortening release cycles.

6. **Inspect and Adapt (I&A):** At the end of each Program Increment, SAFe encourages teams to hold an Inspect and

Adapt workshop. During this event, teams reflect on their performance, identify areas for improvement, and adjust their plans for the next PI.

Roles in SAFe:

SAFe defines various roles, including:

- **Release Train Engineer (RTE):** Responsible for facilitating and supporting the Agile Release Train.

- **Product Owner (PO):** Represents the customer and sets the priorities for the team.

- **Scrum Master (SM):** Ensures the team adheres to agile principles and removes impediments.

- **System Architect (SA):** Provides technical leadership and guidance.

- **Product Manager (PM):** Defines the product vision and roadmap.

Benefits of SAFe:

1. **Scalability:** SAFe is designed to scale agile principles and practices to large organizations with multiple teams and complex projects.

2. **Alignment:** It aligns the organization's strategy with its

execution, ensuring that teams work on high-priority items that deliver value.

3. **Improved Quality:** SAFe promotes technical practices that lead to higher product quality and reliability.

4. **Faster Time to Market:** By adopting Lean and agile practices, SAFe helps organizations deliver value to customers more quickly.

5. **Enhanced Collaboration:** SAFe encourages collaboration and communication across teams and departments.

Challenges of SAFe:

1. **Complexity:** Implementing SAFe can be complex, especially in large organizations with existing processes and structures.

2. **Cultural Change:** SAFe requires a cultural shift towards agile values and principles, which can be challenging for some organizations.

3. **Training and Skill Development:** Teams and leaders need training to fully understand and implement SAFe effectively.

In conclusion, SAFe (Scaled Agile Framework) offers a structured and flexible approach to scaling Agile practices within large organizations. It provides a framework for aligning strategy with execution, delivering value to customers, and fostering a

Lean-Agile mindset across the enterprise. While it comes with challenges, the benefits of SAFe in terms of improved collaboration, faster time to market, and enhanced product quality make it a compelling choice for organizations seeking to navigate the complexities of large-scale agile adoption.

B. LESS (Large-Scale Scrum): Scaling Agile Simplicity for Enterprise Agility

Large-Scale Scrum, often referred to as LeSS, is an Agile framework designed to scale the principles and practices of Scrum for organizations dealing with complex products and projects. LeSS adopts Scrum's core values, roles, events, and artifacts but extends them to encompass multiple teams working on a single product. LeSS strives to retain the simplicity and transparency of Scrum while enabling organizations to collaborate effectively, deliver value to customers, and maintain agility at scale. In this in-depth exploration, we will delve into LeSS, its key principles, components, and how it empowers organizations to achieve enterprise agility.

Key Principles of LeSS:

1. **Minimalism and Simplicity:** LeSS is rooted in the belief that complexity should be minimized. It aims to keep the framework as simple as possible while addressing the challenges of large-scale development.

2. **Transparency:** LeSS promotes transparency at all levels, allowing everyone to have a clear view of the work being done, progress made, and impediments faced.

3. **Empirical Process Control:** Like Scrum, LeSS relies on empiricism, where decisions are based on observation and experimentation rather than speculation.

Key Components of LeSS:

1. **Scrum Roles:** LeSS retains the core Scrum roles of Product Owner, Scrum Master, and Development Team. However, in LeSS, these roles serve the product as a whole, not just individual teams.

2. **Product Backlog:** There is a single Product Backlog for the entire product. It contains all the items needed to deliver value to the customer.

3. **Sprint:** All teams work on synchronized Sprints, with a common Sprint goal. This ensures that all teams are focused on delivering the same business value.

4. **Definition of Done (DoD):** LeSS defines a common DoD for all teams to ensure that the product increment is potentially shippable at the end of each Sprint.

5. **Sprint Review:** LeSS encourages a single Sprint Review, where all teams demonstrate the integrated product increment

to stakeholders.

6. **Sprint Retrospective:** Each team conducts its own Sprint Retrospective, but there can be an overall retrospective to identify improvements at the product level.

7. **Overall Product Backlog Refinement:** While teams may conduct their Backlog Refinement sessions, there is an additional focus on Overall Product Backlog Refinement to ensure that dependencies are addressed.

LeSS Variants:

1. **LeSS Huge:** Designed for organizations with hundreds of people working on a single product, LeSS Huge adds an additional layer of coordination and facilitation.

2. **LeSS Guide:** This variant simplifies the framework further for smaller organizations or those with less complex products.

Benefits of LeSS:

1. **Simplicity:** LeSS maintains the simplicity of Scrum while scaling it effectively, making it easier for teams to adopt and adapt.

2. **Transparency:** With a single Product Backlog and common Sprint goals, LeSS enhances transparency and reduces information silos.

3. **Focus on Value:** LeSS emphasizes delivering value to customers consistently, enabling organizations to respond to market changes faster.

4. **Empowered Teams:** Teams are self-managing and cross-functional, leading to higher autonomy and motivation.

5. **Reduced Waste:** LeSS helps organizations reduce waste by optimizing processes, removing unnecessary roles, and fostering a culture of continuous improvement.

Challenges of LeSS:

1. **Cultural Shift:** Like any Agile framework, LeSS requires a significant cultural shift, which can be challenging for organizations with deeply ingrained traditional practices.

2. **Skill and Knowledge Gap:** Teams and leaders need training and support to understand and implement LeSS effectively.

3. **Dependency Management:** Addressing dependencies across multiple teams can be complex and requires coordination.

In conclusion, Large-Scale Scrum (LeSS) offers a scaled Agile framework that retains the simplicity and transparency of Scrum while enabling organizations to tackle complex product development and projects. It encourages collaboration, transparency, and a focus on delivering value to customers. LeSS variants cater to different organizational sizes and complexities, making it adaptable to a wide range of scenarios. While there are challenges in adopting LeSS, the benefits in terms of agility, transparency, and value delivery make it a compelling choice for organizations striving to achieve enterprise agility.

CHAPTER 17

IT Project Management Metrics and Dashboards: Navigating Data-Driven Success

In today's dynamic IT landscape, successful project management hinges on the ability to gather, analyze, and act upon data effectively. IT Project Management Metrics and Dashboards serve as powerful tools that enable organizations to measure performance, monitor progress, and make informed decisions. These data-driven insights not only enhance project efficiency but also contribute to the achievement of organizational goals. In this introductory exploration, we will delve into the world of IT Project Management Metrics and Dashboards, unveiling their significance, key components, and how they empower project managers to steer their endeavors toward success in an increasingly data-centric environment.

A. Measuring Project Performance: Key Metrics and Strategies for Success

Measuring project performance is a fundamental aspect of effective IT project management. It involves collecting and analyzing data to assess how well a project is progressing, whether it's meeting its objectives, and whether it's delivering value to the organization. By quantifying various aspects of a project's performance, project managers and stakeholders can make informed decisions, identify areas for improvement, and ensure that the project stays on track. In this in-depth exploration, we will delve into the essential aspects of measuring project performance, including key metrics and strategies for success.

Key Metrics for Measuring Project Performance:

1. **Schedule Performance:**

   - **Schedule Variance (SV):** SV measures the difference between the planned and actual progress of the project in terms of time. A positive SV indicates that the project is ahead of schedule, while a negative SV indicates a delay.

   - **Schedule Performance Index (SPI):** SPI is the ratio of the earned value (EV) to the planned value (PV) of the project's schedule. It provides an indication of schedule efficiency.

2. **Cost Performance:**

   - **Cost Variance (CV):** CV measures the difference between the budgeted cost of work performed (EV) and the actual cost of work performed (AC). A positive CV indicates cost savings, while a negative CV indicates cost overruns.

- **Cost Performance Index (CPI):** CPI is the ratio of the EV to the AC. It provides insights into cost efficiency.

3. **Quality Performance:**

- **Defect Density:** Defect density quantifies the number of defects or issues identified per unit of work, such as lines of code or test cases. Lower defect density indicates better quality.

- **Defect Removal Efficiency (DRE):** DRE measures the effectiveness of defect removal processes. It's calculated by dividing the number of defects removed by the total number of defects (including those that weren't removed).

4. **Scope Performance:**

- **Scope Creep:** Scope creep measures the extent to which project requirements or scope have changed since the project began. It's essential to manage scope creep to prevent project delays and budget overruns.

5. **Customer Satisfaction:**

- **Net Promoter Score (NPS):** NPS assesses customer satisfaction by asking customers how likely they are to recommend the product or service to others. Higher NPS scores indicate higher satisfaction.

6. **Risk Performance:**

- **Risk Register Updates:** Regular updates to the risk register, including the identification of new risks, changes in risk assessments, and actions taken to mitigate risks, help in managing project risks effectively.

Strategies for Measuring Project Performance:

1. **Establish Clear Baselines:** Define clear project baselines for schedule, cost, and scope. These baselines serve as benchmarks against which actual performance can be measured.

2. **Regular Reporting:** Implement a regular reporting mechanism to capture and communicate project performance metrics to stakeholders. This includes status reports, dashboards, and key performance indicators (KPIs).

3. **Earned Value Management (EVM):** EVM is a powerful technique for integrating scope, schedule, and cost objectives. It provides a comprehensive view of project performance.

4. **Continuous Monitoring:** Continuously monitor project progress, risks, and issues. Early detection of problems allows

for timely corrective actions.

5. **Feedback Loops:** Establish feedback loops with stakeholders, including customers and team members. Gather their input on project performance and make necessary adjustments.

6. **Quality Assurance:** Implement quality assurance processes and conduct regular quality audits to ensure that project deliverables meet the required standards.

7. **Lessons Learned:** Conduct lessons learned sessions at the end of each project phase or at project completion. Document what worked well and what didn't to inform future projects.

8. **Adaptive Project Management:** Embrace adaptive project management approaches such as Agile or Scrum, which facilitate ongoing evaluation and adaptation of project performance.

9. **Use of Project Management Software:** Utilize project management software and tools that offer real-time tracking and reporting capabilities.

In conclusion, measuring project performance is a critical aspect of IT project management that ensures projects stay on track, meet objectives, and deliver value. Effective measurement involves tracking key metrics, establishing clear baselines, and implementing strategies for continuous monitoring and improvement. By leveraging performance data and insights, organizations can make informed decisions and increase the likelihood of project success.

B. Communicating Performance with Metrics: Effective Project Reporting and Stakeholder Engagement

Effective communication of project performance through metrics is vital for project managers and organizations. Metrics provide a quantitative and objective way to convey how a project is progressing, whether it's meeting its goals, and where improvements may be needed. Clear and timely communication of performance metrics helps stakeholders understand the project's status, make informed decisions, and take corrective actions if necessary. In this in-depth exploration, we will delve into the importance of communicating performance with metrics, best practices for reporting, and how it enhances stakeholder engagement and project success.

Importance of Communicating Performance with Metrics:

1. **Transparency:** Metrics offer a transparent view of the project's status and progress. Stakeholders can see both successes and challenges, fostering trust and accountability.

2. **Informed Decision-Making:** Metrics provide the data needed

for informed decision-making. Whether it's adjusting project priorities, allocating resources, or managing risks, data-driven decisions are more likely to lead to successful outcomes.

3. **Accountability:** Metrics hold project teams and stakeholders accountable for their roles and responsibilities. When performance is measured, individuals are more likely to take ownership of their contributions.

4. **Early Issue Identification:** Metrics allow for the early identification of issues or deviations from the plan. This enables timely corrective actions, reducing the impact on project timelines and budgets.

Best Practices for Communicating Performance with Metrics:

1. **Selecting Relevant Metrics:**

   - Choose metrics that align with project objectives and key performance indicators (KPIs). Focus on metrics that matter most to stakeholders.

   - Metrics should be specific, measurable, achievable, relevant, and time-bound (SMART).

2. **Regular Reporting:**

   - Establish a regular reporting cadence, such as weekly,

bi-weekly, or monthly updates, depending on the project's timeline and complexity.

- Consistency in reporting helps stakeholders anticipate and access project information.

3. **Visualization:**

- Use visual representations of data, such as charts, graphs, and dashboards, to make complex metrics more accessible and understandable.

- Visualizations help stakeholders quickly grasp trends and patterns in the data.

4. **Clear Narrative:**

- Provide context and a clear narrative around the metrics. Explain what the numbers mean, why they are important, and any actions being taken based on the data.

- Avoid jargon or technical language that may be unclear to non-specialist stakeholders.

5. **Benchmarking:**

- Compare project metrics to benchmarks or industry standards when relevant. This helps stakeholders understand how the project is performing relative to expectations.

6. **Highlighting Trends:**

- Identify and highlight trends over time. Are metrics improving, deteriorating, or staying relatively stable? Trends offer valuable insights into project health.

7. **Risk and Issue Reporting:**

- Include metrics related to project risks and issues. This helps stakeholders understand the potential challenges the project faces and how they are being managed.

8. **Engaging Stakeholders:**

- Engage stakeholders in discussions about project performance. Encourage questions, feedback, and collaboration to address issues or seize opportunities.

- Tailor communications to different stakeholder groups, emphasizing the aspects of performance that matter most to them.

Enhancing Stakeholder Engagement:

1. **Empowerment:** When stakeholders are well-informed through clear and relevant metrics, they feel empowered to contribute to project success.

2. **Proactive Problem-Solving:** Early identification of performance issues through metrics allows stakeholders to proactively address challenges, minimizing disruptions.

3. **Alignment:** Metrics help align stakeholders' expectations with project reality. This reduces surprises and improves overall satisfaction.

4. **Accountability:** Clear metrics create a culture of accountability, where all stakeholders are responsible for project success.

5. **Trust:** Transparent and consistent reporting of metrics builds trust among stakeholders, enhancing collaboration and confidence in project leadership.

In conclusion, communicating performance with metrics is a cornerstone of effective project management. It promotes transparency, informed decision-making, and stakeholder engagement. By selecting relevant metrics, adopting best practices in reporting, and actively involving stakeholders in discussions about project performance, organizations can increase the likelihood of project success and achieve their strategic goals.

CHAPTER 18

Advanced Risk Management Techniques: Safeguarding Project Success in an Uncertain World

In the dynamic landscape of IT project management, uncertainties and risks are inherent. To navigate these challenges effectively, project managers and organizations must go beyond conventional risk management approaches. Advanced Risk Management Techniques offer a comprehensive toolkit to identify, assess, mitigate, and even leverage risks to their advantage. In this introductory exploration, we will delve into the world of advanced risk management, unveiling its significance, key methodologies, and how it empowers project professionals to proactively safeguard project success in an increasingly uncertain world.

A. Quantitative Risk Analysis: Harnessing Data for Informed Decision-Making

Quantitative risk analysis is a powerful technique within the realm of advanced risk management that involves using data and mathematical models to assess and quantify project risks. Unlike qualitative risk analysis, which assigns subjective probability and impact values, quantitative analysis relies on objective data, statistical methods, and simulations to provide a more accurate and nuanced understanding of risk exposure. In this in-depth exploration, we will delve into the intricacies of quantitative risk analysis, its key components, benefits, and how it empowers project managers to make informed decisions in the face of uncertainty.

Key Components of Quantitative Risk Analysis:

1. **Risk Data Collection:**

   - The process begins with the collection of historical data, expert judgment, and other relevant information related to the project and its potential risks.

2. **Risk Quantification:**

   - Quantification involves assigning numerical values to risk elements, such as cost and schedule impacts, probabilities, and potential consequences.

3. **Probabilistic Modeling:**

   - Probabilistic models, including Monte Carlo simulations and decision trees, are used to represent and analyze uncertainties in the project. Monte Carlo simulations generate multiple scenarios to assess the range of possible outcomes.

4. **Sensitivity Analysis:**

- Sensitivity analysis identifies which project variables have the most significant impact on overall project outcomes. It helps prioritize risks and focus mitigation efforts.

5. **Expected Monetary Value (EMV):**

- EMV is a key concept in quantitative risk analysis, representing the expected financial impact of risks. It is calculated by multiplying the probability of an event by its associated impact.

Benefits of Quantitative Risk Analysis:

1. **Accuracy and Precision:** Quantitative analysis provides a more precise assessment of risks, reducing the reliance on subjective judgment.

2. **Data-Driven Decision-Making:** Project managers can make decisions based on data and statistical models, increasing confidence in risk mitigation strategies.

3. **Scenario Analysis:** Monte Carlo simulations allow project teams to explore various scenarios and their probabilities, enabling better preparation for potential outcomes.

4. **Cost and Schedule Contingency:** Quantitative analysis helps

determine the appropriate level of contingency reserves needed to address identified risks, preventing overestimation or underestimation.

5. **Risk Prioritization:** By quantifying risks, project managers can prioritize mitigation efforts and resources on the most significant threats to project success.

Steps in Quantitative Risk Analysis:

1. **Risk Identification:** Identify and document potential risks and their characteristics.

2. **Risk Data Gathering:** Collect historical data, expert opinions, and relevant information to quantify risks.

3. **Risk Quantification:** Assign numerical values to risks, including probability distributions for key variables.

4. **Probabilistic Modeling:** Use mathematical models and simulations to assess risk exposure.

5. **Sensitivity Analysis:** Analyze how changes in key variables affect project outcomes.

6. **Expected Monetary Value (EMV) Calculation:** Calculate the expected financial impact of risks.

7. **Risk Response Planning:** Develop risk response strategies based on the analysis, such as risk avoidance, risk mitigation,

risk transfer, or risk acceptance.

8. **Decision-Making:** Use the analysis results to inform project decisions, budgeting, and scheduling.

Challenges of Quantitative Risk Analysis:

1. **Data Availability:** Quantitative analysis relies on data, and obtaining historical project data or relevant industry data can be challenging.

2. **Complexity:** The mathematical and statistical techniques used in quantitative analysis may be complex and require specialized software tools.

3. **Resource Intensive:** Conducting quantitative analysis, especially using Monte Carlo simulations, can be resource-intensive in terms of time and computational power.

4. **Assumptions:** The accuracy of quantitative risk analysis depends on the quality of assumptions made, and uncertainties in these assumptions can affect results.

In conclusion, quantitative risk analysis is a valuable tool that empowers project managers to make data-driven decisions and effectively manage project uncertainties. By using statistical models and simulations, project teams can gain a deeper understanding of the potential risks and their impacts, allowing for more accurate planning and risk mitigation strategies. While it requires effort and expertise, the benefits of increased accuracy and informed decision-making make quantitative risk analysis a critical component of advanced project risk management.

B. Monte Carlo Simulations: Unveiling the Power of Probabilistic Modeling in Risk Analysis

Monte Carlo simulations, named after the famous casino in Monaco, are a sophisticated and widely used technique in quantitative risk analysis and decision-making. These simulations provide a systematic and data-driven approach to assess the uncertainty associated with various project variables, enabling organizations and project managers to make more informed decisions in the face of risk and complexity. In this in-depth exploration, we will delve into the intricacies of Monte Carlo simulations, their principles, applications, benefits, and how they empower organizations to navigate uncertainties with confidence.

Principles of Monte Carlo Simulations:

At its core, Monte Carlo simulation is a statistical technique that relies on randomness and probability to model the behavior of complex systems or processes. The main principles behind Monte Carlo simulations are as follows:

1. **Random Sampling:** Monte Carlo simulations use random

sampling to generate a large number of possible scenarios or outcomes based on probability distributions. These scenarios represent the range of possibilities for the variables being analyzed.

2. **Probability Distributions:** Key variables in the simulation are assigned probability distributions, such as normal, triangular, or uniform distributions. These distributions describe the range of possible values and their likelihood.

3. **Numerical Integration:** The simulation calculates and integrates the results of multiple scenarios to provide statistical summaries and insights into the behavior of the system.

Steps in Performing Monte Carlo Simulations:

1. **Define Variables:** Identify the project variables that are subject to uncertainty and assign probability distributions to them. These variables could include project duration, cost estimates, resource availability, and more.

2. **Generate Random Samples:** Generate a large number of random samples for each variable based on their assigned probability distributions. This involves creating a dataset of potential values for each variable.

3. **Run Scenarios:** For each random sample of variable values, run the project simulation. This may involve calculations that

use the variable values to estimate project outcomes.

4. **Collect Data:** Collect data on project outcomes from each scenario, such as project completion time, cost, or other performance metrics.

5. **Analyze Results:** Analyze the collected data to generate probabilistic information about the project, such as the probability of meeting a certain deadline or staying within budget.

6. **Make Informed Decisions:** Use the insights gained from the Monte Carlo simulation to make informed decisions, allocate resources, develop risk mitigation strategies, or set contingency plans.

Applications of Monte Carlo Simulations:

Monte Carlo simulations find applications across various domains, including:

1. **Project Management:** Assessing project schedules, cost estimates, and risk exposure to determine the likelihood of on-time and on-budget completion.

2. **Finance:** Analyzing investment portfolios, evaluating the risk-return trade-off, and estimating the potential value at risk (VaR) of financial assets.

3. **Manufacturing and Quality Control:** Analyzing manufacturing processes to optimize production, predicting defect rates, and assessing the reliability of products.

4. **Engineering:** Evaluating structural integrity, analyzing fluid dynamics, and simulating the behavior of complex systems.

5. **Supply Chain Management:** Assessing supply chain risks, optimizing inventory levels, and evaluating the impact of disruptions.

Benefits of Monte Carlo Simulations:

1. **Comprehensive Risk Assessment:** Monte Carlo simulations provide a comprehensive assessment of risk by considering multiple variables and their interdependencies.

2. **Data-Driven Decision-Making:** Simulations are based on data and statistics, leading to more informed and objective decision-making.

3. **Scenario Exploration:** Simulations enable the exploration of various scenarios, helping organizations prepare for a range of possible outcomes.

4. **Quantification of Risk:** The simulations provide quantifiable metrics, such as the probability of success or failure, which can guide risk management strategies.

5. **Cost-Effective Risk Analysis:** Monte Carlo simulations allow organizations to perform risk analysis without the need for costly and time-consuming real-world experiments.

Challenges of Monte Carlo Simulations:

1. **Data Availability:** Obtaining accurate and relevant data for probability distributions can be challenging.

2. **Complexity:** Setting up and running Monte Carlo simulations can be complex and require specialized software and expertise.

3. **Interdependencies:** Capturing and modeling the interdependencies between variables accurately can be challenging.

4. **Computational Resources:** Performing a large number of simulations may require significant computational resources and time.

In conclusion, Monte Carlo simulations are a powerful tool for organizations and project managers to assess and manage uncertainty and risk. By simulating a wide range of possible scenarios and outcomes, organizations can make informed decisions, allocate resources effectively, and develop robust risk management strategies. While they require careful planning and expertise, the benefits of enhanced decision-making and risk mitigation make Monte Carlo simulations a valuable asset in a world characterized by uncertainty.

CHAPTER 19

Cybersecurity in Project Management: Safeguarding Digital Assets and Project Success

In an increasingly digital and interconnected world, the integration of cybersecurity into project management has become imperative. Cyber threats pose a significant risk to projects, potentially compromising data, infrastructure, and organizational reputation. Therefore, understanding and implementing robust cybersecurity measures within the project management framework is essential for safeguarding digital assets and ensuring project success. In this introductory exploration, we will delve into the critical role of cybersecurity in project management, its importance, key considerations, and how it forms a crucial layer of protection in today's project landscape.

A. Integrating Cybersecurity into Projects: A Comprehensive Approach to Risk Mitigation

Cybersecurity has evolved from being a standalone concern for IT departments to a critical component of project management across various industries. As cyber threats continue to evolve in sophistication and frequency, organizations must take a proactive approach to integrate cybersecurity seamlessly into their projects.

This ensures that sensitive data, systems, and operations remain protected throughout the project's lifecycle. In this in-depth exploration, we will delve into the strategies and best practices for integrating cybersecurity into projects effectively, safeguarding digital assets, and mitigating cyber risks.

Why Integrate Cybersecurity into Projects?

1. **Protection of Digital Assets:** Projects often involve the creation, storage, and transfer of valuable digital assets, such as sensitive data, intellectual property, and proprietary software. Integrating cybersecurity safeguards these assets from theft, espionage, or unauthorized access.

2. **Risk Mitigation:** Cyber threats, including data breaches, ransomware attacks, and malware infections, pose significant risks to project success. Integrating cybersecurity allows organizations to proactively identify and mitigate these risks, reducing the potential for disruptions and financial losses.

3. **Regulatory Compliance:** Many industries are subject to stringent cybersecurity regulations and data protection laws. Failure to comply can result in severe penalties. Integrating cybersecurity ensures that projects adhere to these requirements from the outset.

4. **Brand Reputation:** A cybersecurity breach can tarnish an organization's reputation. By integrating cybersecurity into

projects, companies demonstrate their commitment to protecting customer data and maintaining trust.

Strategies for Integrating Cybersecurity into Projects:

1. **Risk Assessment and Planning:**

   - Begin by conducting a comprehensive risk assessment to identify potential cybersecurity threats and vulnerabilities specific to the project.

   - Develop a cybersecurity plan that outlines security objectives, risk mitigation strategies, and roles and responsibilities.

2. **Security by Design:**

   - Implement the principle of "security by design" from the project's inception. This involves considering cybersecurity at every stage of project development.

   - Incorporate security controls, such as access controls, encryption, and secure coding practices, into project requirements and design.

3. **Data Protection:**

   - Encrypt sensitive data both at rest and in transit. Ensure that data is securely stored, transmitted, and disposed of when no longer needed.

- Establish data classification and handling procedures to determine how different types of data should be protected.

4. **Access Control:**

   - Implement strong authentication mechanisms and access controls to ensure that only authorized personnel can access project resources and data.

   - Enforce the principle of least privilege, granting users only the minimum access necessary to perform their roles.

5. **Security Awareness and Training:**

   - Conduct cybersecurity training and awareness programs for project teams. Ensure that team members are well-informed about cybersecurity best practices and potential threats.

6. **Incident Response and Recovery:**

   - Develop an incident response plan that outlines how to detect, respond to, and recover from cybersecurity incidents. Test the plan through tabletop exercises.

   - Establish communication protocols to report security incidents promptly.

7. **Third-Party Risk Management:**

- Assess the cybersecurity posture of third-party vendors and service providers involved in the project. Ensure that they meet your organization's security standards.

8. **Continuous Monitoring:**

- Implement continuous monitoring of project assets and systems to detect and respond to emerging threats in real-time.

- Use security information and event management (SIEM) systems to centralize and analyze security data.

9. **Documentation and Compliance:**

- Maintain thorough documentation of cybersecurity measures, assessments, and incident responses.

- Regularly review and update cybersecurity policies and procedures to stay in compliance with evolving regulations.

Challenges of Integrating Cybersecurity into Projects:

1. **Resource Constraints:** Limited budgets and resources can hinder the implementation of robust cybersecurity measures.

2. **Complexity:** Integrating cybersecurity into projects may introduce complexity, potentially impacting project timelines and budgets.

3. **Resistance to Change:** Project teams may resist cybersecurity measures if they perceive them as cumbersome or disruptive to their workflows.

4. **Skill Shortages:** Finding qualified cybersecurity professionals to support project efforts can be challenging, given the high demand for cybersecurity expertise.

In conclusion, integrating cybersecurity into projects is not just a necessity; it's a strategic imperative. By adopting a proactive and comprehensive approach to cybersecurity, organizations can protect their digital assets, maintain regulatory compliance, and reduce the risk of cyber incidents that could disrupt projects and damage their reputation. It's an investment in both project success and long-term security.

B. Protecting Sensitive Data in IT Projects: Strategies for Data Security and Compliance

In today's digital landscape, sensitive data is the lifeblood of many organizations. IT projects often involve the creation, processing, or storage of such data, making data security a paramount concern. The consequences of data breaches, ranging from financial losses to damage to reputation, emphasize the importance of safeguarding sensitive information throughout the project lifecycle. In this in-depth exploration, we will delve into strategies, best practices, and technologies for protecting sensitive data in IT projects, ensuring both security and regulatory compliance.

Understanding Sensitive Data:

Sensitive data encompasses a wide range of information that, if exposed or compromised, could harm individuals, organizations, or even national security. It includes:

1. **Personal Data:** Information like names, addresses, social security numbers, and medical records.

2. **Financial Data:** Credit card numbers, bank account details, and financial transactions.

3. **Intellectual Property:** Proprietary information, trade secrets, patents, and copyrights.

4. **Healthcare Data:** Protected health information (PHI) governed by regulations such as HIPAA.

5. **Corporate Data:** Business plans, customer lists, and strategic data.

Strategies for Protecting Sensitive Data in IT Projects:

1. **Data Classification:**

    - Begin by classifying data based on its sensitivity. Assign labels like "confidential," "internal use only," or "public" to clearly define access and handling requirements.

2. **Access Control:**

    - Implement strong access controls to ensure that only authorized personnel can access sensitive data.

    - Enforce role-based access control (RBAC) to restrict access based on job roles and responsibilities.

3. **Encryption:**

    - Encrypt sensitive data both at rest and in transit. Use strong encryption algorithms to protect data from unauthorized access.

4. **Data Masking and Redaction:**

    - In non-production environments, mask or redact sensitive data to prevent exposure during development, testing, or training.

5. **Secure Storage:**

   - Utilize secure data storage solutions, such as encrypted databases and secure file systems, to protect data at rest.

6. **Secure Development Practices:**

   - Incorporate secure coding practices to prevent vulnerabilities that could be exploited to access sensitive data.

   - Conduct code reviews and security testing to identify and remediate vulnerabilities.

7. **Regular Auditing and Monitoring:**

   - Implement continuous monitoring and auditing of systems and data access to detect and respond to security incidents in real-time.

   - Utilize intrusion detection systems (IDS) and intrusion prevention systems (IPS).

8. **Secure Data Transmission:**

   - Use secure communication protocols (e.g., HTTPS, SFTP, VPNs) to protect data in transit.

9. **Data Backup and Recovery:**

- Regularly back up sensitive data and establish disaster recovery plans to ensure data availability in case of a breach or system failure.

10. **User Training and Awareness:**

- Educate project teams and users about data security best practices, including the handling of sensitive data and the recognition of phishing attempts.

11. **Regulatory Compliance:**

- Familiarize yourself with relevant data protection regulations, such as GDPR, HIPAA, or CCPA, and ensure project compliance.

- Develop and document policies and procedures to meet regulatory requirements.

12. **Secure Vendor and Third-Party Relationships:**

- Assess the security measures of third-party vendors and service providers who have access to sensitive data. Ensure they comply with your security standards.

Data Security Technologies:

1. **Data Loss Prevention (DLP) Solutions:** DLP tools help organizations monitor, detect, and prevent unauthorized data access or leakage.

2. **Data Encryption:** Utilize encryption tools and libraries to secure data both in transit and at rest.

3. **Authentication and Access Management:** Implement strong authentication mechanisms, multi-factor authentication (MFA), and identity and access management (IAM) solutions.

4. **Security Information and Event Management (SIEM):** SIEM platforms collect and analyze security data, providing real-time insights into potential threats.

5. **Endpoint Security:** Employ endpoint security solutions, including antivirus software and endpoint detection and response (EDR) tools, to protect devices and data.

Challenges in Protecting Sensitive Data:

1. **Complexity:** Ensuring data security can be complex, especially in large and distributed IT environments.

2. **User Error:** Many data breaches result from human error, such as misconfigured security settings or accidental data exposure.

3. **Evolving Threat Landscape:** Cyber threats are continually evolving, requiring organizations to adapt their security measures accordingly.

4. **Regulatory Compliance:** Meeting the requirements of various data protection regulations can be challenging and resource-intensive.

In conclusion, protecting sensitive data in IT projects is a multifaceted effort that combines technology, policies, and best practices. By implementing robust security measures, regularly auditing and monitoring data access, and ensuring compliance with relevant regulations, organizations can mitigate the risk of data breaches and safeguard their most valuable assets throughout the project lifecycle. Data security is not just a technical concern; it is a critical aspect of responsible and ethical project management.

CHAPTER 20

Legal and Contractual Aspects in IT Project Management: Navigating the Legal Landscape

In the realm of IT project management, legal and contractual aspects play a pivotal role in defining the relationships, responsibilities, and outcomes of projects. These aspects encompass a broad spectrum of legal considerations, ranging from project contracts and intellectual property rights to dispute resolution and compliance with regulatory frameworks. Understanding and effectively managing these legal and contractual dimensions are essential for ensuring project success and minimizing potential legal pitfalls. In this introductory exploration, we will delve into the critical significance of legal and contractual aspects in IT project management, shedding light on their implications and the strategies required to navigate the complex legal landscape effectively.

A. Legal Considerations in IT Project Contracts: Mitigating Risks and Ensuring Success

Contracts form the foundation of IT project management, outlining the rights, responsibilities, and obligations of all parties involved. Within the context of IT projects, contracts serve as legal documents that not only define project scope and deliverables but also address various legal considerations. Understanding and addressing these legal aspects is essential to mitigate risks, protect intellectual property, and ensure the successful execution of IT projects. In this in-depth exploration, we will delve into the critical legal considerations within IT project contracts and the strategies for managing them effectively.

Key Legal Considerations in IT Project Contracts:

1. **Scope of Work:**

   - A well-defined scope of work is essential in IT project contracts. It outlines the project's objectives, tasks, and deliverables, ensuring both parties have a clear understanding of project expectations.

2. **Payment Terms:**

   - Payment terms should be clearly defined, including milestones, invoicing schedules, and payment methods. This ensures that compensation aligns with project progress.

3. **Intellectual Property Rights (IPR):**

   - Specify ownership and licensing of intellectual property, including software, code, designs, and any project-related creations. This is crucial for protecting the interests of both the client and the service provider.

4. **Confidentiality and Non-Disclosure:**

   - Contracts often include clauses that require parties to maintain the confidentiality of sensitive information. Non-disclosure agreements (NDAs) may be necessary to protect proprietary data.

5. **Liability and Indemnification:**

   - Define the liability of each party for breaches, errors, or omissions. Indemnification clauses allocate responsibility and liability in case of legal claims or disputes.

6. **Termination Clauses:**

   - Specify conditions under which the contract can be terminated, such as non-performance, breach of contract, or changes in project scope.

7. **Dispute Resolution:**

   - Detail the process for resolving disputes, which may include negotiation, mediation, arbitration, or litigation. This prevents costly and time-consuming legal battles.

8. **Force Majeure:**

   - Address unforeseeable events, such as natural disasters or acts of God, that may impact project timelines and deliverables.

9. **Regulatory Compliance:**

   - Ensure that the project and contract adhere to relevant legal and regulatory requirements, such as data protection laws, export control regulations, or industry-specific standards.

10. **Change Management:**

   - Define how changes to project scope, requirements, or timelines will be managed and approved, preventing scope creep and disputes.

11. **Insurance Coverage:**

   - Evaluate whether project-specific insurance coverage, such as professional liability insurance, is necessary to mitigate risks.

Strategies for Managing Legal Considerations in IT Project Contracts:

1. **Legal Expertise:**

    *   Involve legal counsel with expertise in IT and technology contracts to draft, review, and negotiate contracts. Legal professionals can identify potential risks and ensure compliance with relevant laws.

2. **Clear and Specific Language:**

    *   Use precise and unambiguous language in contracts to eliminate misunderstandings and ambiguities.

3. **Thorough Due Diligence:**

    *   Conduct due diligence on all parties involved, including background checks and financial assessments, to ensure they can fulfill their contractual obligations.

4. **Regular Review and Updates:**

    *   Contracts should be living documents that are regularly reviewed and updated as project circumstances change.

5. **Documentation:**

- Maintain thorough documentation of all communications, changes, and project-related decisions. This can be invaluable in case of disputes.

6. **Communication:**

- Foster open and transparent communication between all parties throughout the project to address issues promptly and prevent conflicts from escalating.

7. **Compliance Monitoring:**

- Establish processes to monitor and ensure ongoing compliance with contractual obligations and regulatory requirements.

8. **Risk Mitigation Plans:**

- Develop risk mitigation plans that outline how potential risks and issues will be addressed to minimize their impact on the project.

Challenges in Managing Legal Considerations:

1. **Complexity:** The legal aspects of IT project contracts can be complex and require specialized legal knowledge.

2. **Changing Regulations:** Rapid changes in technology and

data privacy regulations mean that contracts must adapt to evolving legal landscapes.

3. **Negotiation:** Negotiating contract terms can be time-consuming and may involve significant back-and-forth between parties.

4. **Resource Constraints:** Smaller organizations or startups may have limited resources for legal counsel and may need to carefully balance legal considerations with budget constraints.

In conclusion, legal considerations within IT project contracts are a critical aspect of project management. By carefully addressing these legal elements, organizations can mitigate risks, protect their intellectual property, and establish a solid foundation for successful project execution. Legal expertise and clear, well-drafted contracts are essential to navigate the complexities of IT project management within the bounds of the law.

B. Intellectual Property Rights and SLAs in IT Project Contracts: Safeguarding Innovation and Performance

In the realm of IT project contracts, two critical elements often take center stage: Intellectual Property Rights (IPR) and Service Level Agreements (SLAs). These components are pivotal for defining the ownership, protection, and performance expectations surrounding project deliverables. Understanding how to navigate IPR and SLAs effectively is essential for safeguarding innovation, ensuring contractual compliance, and achieving the desired project outcomes. In this in-depth exploration, we will delve into the intricate aspects of Intellectual Property Rights and Service Level Agreements within IT project contracts and their significance in the ever-evolving digital landscape.

Intellectual Property Rights (IPR) in IT Project Contracts:

Intellectual Property Rights pertain to the ownership and rights associated with creations of the mind, which can include software code, designs, inventions, trademarks, and more. In IT project contracts, IPR plays a crucial role in determining who owns, controls, and can use the intellectual property developed during the project. Key considerations include:

1. **Ownership:** Defining whether the client or the service provider retains ownership of the intellectual property created during the project. This includes software code, algorithms, designs, and other creative or innovative work.

2. **Licensing:** When the client retains ownership, licensing terms must be established. These terms dictate how the intellectual property can be used, modified, or sublicensed by the client or other parties.

3. **Open Source Software:** Addressing the use of open source

software in the project and ensuring compliance with open source licenses. This is crucial to avoid legal disputes and maintain transparency.

4. **Confidentiality:** Specifying confidentiality obligations to protect sensitive intellectual property and trade secrets during and after the project.

5. **Third-Party Rights:** Ensuring that the project does not infringe on the intellectual property rights of third parties. This involves conducting thorough intellectual property due diligence.

Service Level Agreements (SLAs) in IT Project Contracts:

Service Level Agreements are contractual commitments that define the expected levels of service quality, performance, and availability. In IT project contracts, SLAs establish the performance benchmarks and accountability of the service provider. Key considerations include:

1. **Performance Metrics:** Defining specific performance metrics, such as response times, uptime percentages, and error rates, that the service provider must meet.

2. **Penalties and Remedies:** Outlining penalties or remedies in case of SLA breaches, such as financial penalties or service credits to the client.

3. **Service Availability:** Specifying the expected availability of IT systems and services, particularly for critical applications and infrastructure.

4. **Incident Response and Resolution:** Describing the procedures for reporting, tracking, and resolving service incidents, including escalation processes.

5. **Change Management:** Addressing how changes to the project or services will be managed, including how they might impact SLAs.

6. **Disaster Recovery and Backup:** Ensuring that the service provider has robust disaster recovery and backup plans in place to minimize downtime and data loss.

Strategies for Managing IPR and SLAs in IT Project Contracts:

1. **Clear Definitions:** Ensure that IPR ownership and SLA terms are clearly defined in the contract, leaving no room for ambiguity.

2. **Legal Counsel:** Engage legal experts with expertise in intellectual property and contract law to review and draft contract terms related to IPR and SLAs.

3. **Due Diligence:** Conduct thorough due diligence on third-party intellectual property rights and the service provider's

capabilities and track record.

4. **Benchmarking:** Use industry benchmarks and standards to set realistic SLA targets and metrics.

5. **Regular Monitoring:** Continuously monitor SLA performance and intellectual property rights throughout the project's duration.

6. **Documentation:** Maintain detailed documentation of IPR and SLA-related activities, including changes, incidents, and dispute resolutions.

Challenges in Managing IPR and SLAs:

1. **Complexity:** The legal intricacies of IPR and SLAs can be complex and require specialized expertise.

2. **Balancing Interests:** Balancing the interests of the client and the service provider can be challenging, particularly when it comes to IPR ownership and SLA enforcement.

3. **Changing Technology:** Rapid technological advancements may require frequent updates and revisions to IPR and SLA terms.

4. **Enforcement:** Enforcing IPR and SLA terms, especially across international boundaries, can be challenging and costly.

In conclusion, Intellectual Property Rights and Service Level

Agreements are vital components of IT project contracts that require careful consideration and management. By addressing these aspects effectively, organizations can protect their intellectual property, ensure service quality, and reduce the risk of legal disputes, contributing to the successful execution of IT projects in the dynamic and innovation-driven digital landscape.

C. Dispute Resolution in IT Project Contracts: Strategies for Effective Conflict Management

In the world of IT project management, conflicts and disputes can arise for various reasons, including disagreements over project scope, delays, performance issues, or contractual breaches. To ensure the successful resolution of such disputes and the continued progress of IT projects, a well-defined and robust dispute resolution process is essential. In this in-depth exploration, we will delve into the intricacies of dispute resolution in IT project contracts, examining the various methods, best practices, and strategies for effectively managing and resolving conflicts.

Methods of Dispute Resolution:

1. **Negotiation:**

   - **Description:** Negotiation is the most common and least formal method of dispute resolution. Parties involved in the dispute engage in discussions to reach a mutually acceptable solution.

- **Use Cases:** Negotiation is suitable for resolving minor conflicts and disagreements when both parties are willing to collaborate and compromise.

- **Best Practices:** Maintain open and respectful communication, focus on shared interests, and be prepared to make concessions to reach an agreement.

2. **Mediation:**

- **Description:** Mediation involves the appointment of a neutral third party (the mediator) to facilitate discussions and help the parties reach a resolution. The mediator does not impose decisions but guides the process.

- **Use Cases:** Mediation is useful when negotiations stall, and parties need assistance in finding common ground. It can be less adversarial than litigation.

- **Best Practices:** Choose a qualified and experienced mediator, establish ground rules for the mediation process, and ensure confidentiality.

3. **Arbitration:**

- **Description:** Arbitration is a more formal process where an independent arbitrator or panel of arbitrators makes a binding decision on the dispute. It is akin to a private, out-of-court trial.

- **Use Cases:** Arbitration is often specified in contracts as the preferred method of dispute resolution. It is suitable for complex disputes where a swift resolution is desired.

- **Best Practices:** Define the arbitration process in the contract, including the selection of arbitrators and the rules governing the proceedings.

4. **Litigation:**

- **Description:** Litigation involves taking the dispute to court, where a judge or jury renders a legally binding judgment.

- **Use Cases:** Litigation is typically the last resort when other methods fail. It can be time-consuming and costly.

- **Best Practices:** Engage legal counsel experienced in IT contract law, gather all relevant evidence, and prepare a strong legal case.

Strategies for Effective Dispute Resolution in IT Projects:

1. **Clear Contractual Provisions:**

   - Ensure that the IT project contract includes detailed clauses outlining the dispute resolution process, including the method (e.g., mediation, arbitration), the selection of neutral parties, and the governing law.

2. **Documentation:**

   - Maintain comprehensive records of all project-related communications, agreements, changes, and issues. This documentation can be invaluable in resolving disputes.

3. **Early Identification and Escalation:**

   - Identify potential issues and conflicts early in the project and address them promptly. If conflicts escalate, follow the prescribed escalation process in the contract.

4. **Legal Expertise:**

   - Engage legal counsel with expertise in IT contract law to navigate complex legal matters and ensure that your rights and interests are protected.

5. **Alternative Dispute Resolution (ADR):**

   • Encourage the use of alternative dispute resolution methods (e.g., negotiation, mediation) before resorting to more adversarial processes like litigation.

6. **Maintain Open Communication:**

   • Foster transparent and open communication between all parties involved in the dispute. Effective communication can often lead to resolution without formal intervention.

7. **Confidentiality Agreements:**

   • Consider including confidentiality agreements in the dispute resolution process to protect sensitive information shared during discussions.

Challenges in Dispute Resolution:

1. **Complexity of IT Projects:** IT projects often involve intricate technical details and dependencies, making dispute resolution more challenging.

2. **Resource Intensiveness:** Legal proceedings, such as litigation and arbitration, can be costly and time-consuming, diverting resources away from the project.

3. **Cross-Border Disputes:** International IT projects may

involve parties from different jurisdictions, complicating the choice of law and jurisdiction for dispute resolution.

4. **Emotional Factors:** Emotions can run high during disputes, making it challenging to maintain a productive and respectful dialogue.

In conclusion, effective dispute resolution is a critical component of IT project management. By establishing clear contractual provisions, maintaining open communication, and leveraging alternative dispute resolution methods when appropriate, organizations can navigate conflicts and disputes successfully, minimize project disruptions, and uphold their contractual obligations in the dynamic world of IT projects.

CHAPTER 21

International and Cross-Cultural Project Management: Navigating Global Challenges

In an increasingly interconnected world, the realm of project management extends beyond geographical borders. International and cross-cultural project management involves the complex task of overseeing projects that span multiple countries, regions, and cultures. These projects present unique challenges and opportunities, from differences in language and communication styles to variations in business practices and regulatory environments. In this introductory exploration, we will delve into the dynamic and diverse landscape of international and cross-cultural project management, shedding light on the strategies and best practices required to successfully navigate global projects.

A. Challenges of Global Project Management: Navigating the Complexities of International Projects

Global project management, which involves overseeing projects that span multiple countries, presents a host of unique challenges that project managers must navigate effectively to ensure success. While these international projects offer

329

opportunities for innovation and growth, they are also accompanied by complexities stemming from diverse cultures, time zones, languages, regulatory environments, and communication barriers. In this in-depth exploration, we will delve into the multifaceted challenges of global project management and provide insights into how to address them proactively.

1. Cultural Diversity:

Challenge: Managing diverse project teams with members from different cultural backgrounds can lead to misunderstandings, miscommunication, and clashes in work styles and values.

Strategies:

- **Cultural Awareness Training:** Provide cultural sensitivity training to team members to enhance their understanding of diverse perspectives.

- **Effective Communication:** Foster open and clear communication channels, considering cultural nuances in language and non-verbal cues.

- **Diversity and Inclusion Policies:** Implement policies that promote diversity and inclusion within the project team.

2. Time Zone Differences:

Challenge: Coordinating activities and meetings across multiple time zones can lead to delays, difficulties in scheduling, and challenges in real-time collaboration.

Strategies:

- **Flexible Scheduling:** Adopt flexible scheduling practices that accommodate team members' time zones.

- **Use of Technology:** Leverage technology tools like project management software and virtual meeting platforms to bridge time zone gaps.

- **Shared Calendars:** Encourage team members to maintain shared calendars to coordinate availability.

3. Language Barriers:

Challenge: Language differences can lead to miscommunication, misunderstandings, and errors in project documentation.

Strategies:

- **Language Skills:** Identify team members with strong language skills and utilize translation services when necessary.

- **Document Translation:** Translate critical project documents and communications into the languages spoken by team members.

- **Clear Communication:** Promote clear and concise communication to minimize language-related challenges.

4. Regulatory and Legal Compliance:

Challenge: Navigating diverse legal and regulatory environments, including taxation, data protection, and intellectual property laws, can be complex and require careful compliance.

Strategies:

- **Legal Expertise:** Engage legal counsel with expertise in international law and compliance.

- **Local Partnerships:** Consider partnerships or collaborations with local firms or experts to navigate specific regulatory requirements.

- **Comprehensive Research:** Conduct thorough research on relevant international laws and regulations.

5. Remote Team Management:

Challenge: Managing remote teams across borders can result in reduced visibility into team performance, potential misalignment with project goals, and challenges in team cohesion.

Strategies:

- **Remote Tools:** Utilize project management software, video conferencing, and collaboration tools to enhance remote team collaboration and monitoring.

- **Regular Check-Ins:** Schedule regular virtual meetings to keep remote team members engaged and informed.

- **Clearly Defined Roles:** Ensure that roles and responsibilities are clearly defined to minimize ambiguity.

6. Currency and Financial Management:

Challenge: Dealing with multiple currencies, exchange rates, and financial systems can complicate budgeting, financial tracking, and procurement.

Strategies:

- **Currency Management Tools:** Use financial management software that can handle multiple currencies and provide real-time exchange rate information.

- **Hedging Strategies:** Implement currency hedging strategies to mitigate currency exchange risks.

- **Expert Financial Advice:** Seek financial advice from experts familiar with international financial regulations.

7. Political and Geopolitical Risks:

Challenge: Political instability, trade disputes, and geopolitical tensions can impact the stability and success of global projects.

Strategies:

- **Risk Assessment:** Conduct a thorough risk assessment that includes political and geopolitical factors.

- **Contingency Planning:** Develop contingency plans to address potential disruptions caused by political events.

- **Global Partnerships:** Forge partnerships with local entities to navigate political challenges.

8. Security Concerns:

Challenge: Ensuring the security of project data and intellectual property when working across borders requires robust cybersecurity measures.

Strategies:

- **Data Encryption:** Implement strong data encryption protocols to protect sensitive information.

- **Access Control:** Enforce stringent access control measures to restrict unauthorized access.

- **Cybersecurity Training:** Provide cybersecurity training to all team members to prevent security breaches.

Navigating the challenges of global project management demands adaptability, cultural sensitivity, and a proactive approach. By leveraging effective communication, technology, local expertise, and comprehensive planning, project managers can mitigate these challenges and unlock the potential benefits of international projects while minimizing risks and disruptions.

B. Best Practices in Cross-Cultural Teams: Fostering Collaboration and Productivity

Cross-cultural teams, composed of individuals from diverse cultural backgrounds, offer a wealth of perspectives and talents. However, they also present unique challenges related to communication, collaboration, and understanding. Effectively managing and leveraging the diversity within cross-cultural teams is essential for achieving success in international projects and organizations. In this in-depth exploration, we will delve into the best practices for promoting cohesion, communication, and productivity in cross-cultural teams.

1. Cultural Awareness and Training:

Practice: Prioritize cultural awareness and training for team members.

Explanation: To bridge cultural gaps, team members should understand the cultural norms, values, and communication styles of their colleagues. Providing cultural sensitivity training can enhance mutual understanding and respect.

2. Effective Communication:

Practice: Promote clear and open communication within the team.

Explanation: Encourage team members to express themselves clearly and respectfully, emphasizing active listening and the importance of asking for clarification when needed. Create an environment where team members feel comfortable sharing their thoughts and concerns.

3. Common Language:

Practice: Establish a common language for communication, if possible.

Explanation: If team members have different native languages, identify a common language for official communications and documentation. While many global teams use English, ensure that language proficiency is sufficient for effective communication.

4. Multilingual Resources:

Practice: Provide multilingual resources when necessary.

Explanation: In cases where team members are more comfortable communicating in their native languages, offer translation and interpretation services. This can improve clarity and reduce misunderstandings.

5. Regular Team Building:

Practice: Organize regular team-building activities.

Explanation: Team-building exercises and social events can help build trust and rapport among team members. These activities can be especially beneficial for cross-cultural teams, as they foster a sense of unity and camaraderie.

6. Clearly Defined Roles and Responsibilities:

Practice: Ensure that roles and responsibilities are clearly defined.

Explanation: Ambiguity in roles can lead to misunderstandings and conflicts. Clearly outlining each team member's responsibilities and expectations helps prevent these issues.

7. Cross-Cultural Training for Leadership:

Practice: Provide cross-cultural training for team leaders and managers.

Explanation: Leaders should lead by example in promoting cultural sensitivity and effective cross-cultural communication. Training can help them better understand the challenges their team members face.

8. Flexible Work Practices:

Practice: Be flexible in accommodating different work practices and time zones.

Explanation: Recognize that team members may have different working hours and practices. Be accommodating and find ways to balance these differences to ensure everyone's contributions are valued.

9. Cultural Celebrations:

Practice: Celebrate cultural holidays and traditions within the team.

Explanation: Acknowledging and celebrating cultural holidays and traditions can promote inclusivity and show respect for diverse backgrounds.

10. Conflict Resolution Procedures:

Practice: Establish clear conflict resolution procedures.

Explanation: Conflicts may arise in cross-cultural teams due to misunderstandings or cultural differences. Having established procedures for addressing and resolving conflicts can prevent these issues from escalating.

11. Feedback and Continuous Improvement:

Practice: Encourage open and constructive feedback.

Explanation: Regularly solicit feedback from team members on how cross-cultural collaboration can be improved. Use this feedback to make continuous improvements to team dynamics and processes.

12. Cultural Sensitivity in Decision-Making:

Practice: Be culturally sensitive in decision-making.

Explanation: When making decisions that impact the team, consider cultural differences and perspectives. Avoid decisions that may inadvertently marginalize or exclude certain team members.

13. Inclusive Leadership:

Practice: Promote inclusive leadership.

Explanation: Leaders should actively involve all team members in decision-making processes and ensure that diverse voices are heard and valued.

Challenges in Cross-Cultural Teams:

1. **Communication Barriers:** Language differences and varying

communication styles can lead to misunderstandings.

2. **Cultural Sensitivity:** Sensitivity to cultural differences is essential but may require ongoing effort and education.

3. **Time Zone Challenges:** Coordinating meetings and collaboration across time zones can be challenging.

4. **Conflict Resolution:** Resolving conflicts arising from cultural misunderstandings requires skill and patience.

5. **Work-Life Balance:** Different cultural attitudes towards work-life balance may need to be considered and accommodated.

In conclusion, cross-cultural teams offer unique opportunities for innovation and creativity but require deliberate efforts to foster collaboration and understanding. By implementing these best practices and acknowledging the challenges, organizations can harness the full potential of their diverse teams and thrive in the global marketplace.

CHAPTER 22

IT Project Management Case Studies: Real-World Insights into Success and Challenges

IT project management is a dynamic field with a multitude of approaches, methodologies, and strategies. While theoretical knowledge is essential, real-world case studies provide invaluable insights into the practical application of IT project management principles. In this introductory exploration, we delve into the world of IT project management case studies, where we examine real projects, their successes, failures, and the lessons they offer. These case studies offer a window into the complexities and triumphs of managing IT projects, shedding light on best practices, innovative solutions, and the strategies needed to overcome obstacles in the ever-evolving technology landscape.

A. Real-world Examples of Successful IT Projects: Lessons in Excellence

Successful IT projects are not just a testament to effective project management but also exemplify innovation, teamwork, and strategic planning. These projects, often characterized by their ability to meet or exceed objectives within budget and time constraints, provide valuable lessons for organizations embarking on similar endeavors. In this in-depth exploration, we will delve into real-world examples of successful IT projects, dissecting the key factors that contributed to their triumph and extracting valuable insights that can guide future projects.

1. NASA's Mars Rover Missions:

Overview: NASA's Mars Rover missions, including the Spirit, Opportunity, and Curiosity rovers, stand as shining examples of complex and successful IT projects. These missions involved the design, construction, and operation of robotic vehicles sent to explore the Martian surface.

Success Factors:

- **Precise Planning:** Meticulous planning, including risk assessment and contingency planning, was integral to the success of these missions.

- **Cross-functional Teams:** Collaboration among scientists, engineers, and IT experts ensured that the rovers could adapt to unforeseen challenges.

- **Iterative Development:** The rovers' software and hardware underwent iterative development to accommodate changing conditions and evolving objectives.

2. The Affordable Care Act (ACA) Healthcare.gov Project:

Overview: While initially plagued by technical issues, Healthcare.gov, the online marketplace for health insurance under the Affordable Care Act, underwent a remarkable transformation to become a successful IT project.

Success Factors:

- **Swift Remediation:** After the initial technical challenges, a dedicated team of experts worked tirelessly to address issues promptly.

- **User-Centric Approach:** Redesign efforts focused on improving the user experience, resulting in a more user-friendly platform.

- **Collaboration with Private Sector:** The government collaborated with private-sector tech companies to leverage their expertise in resolving technical challenges.

3. The London Olympics IT Infrastructure:

Overview: The IT infrastructure for the 2012 London Olympics was a massive undertaking, involving the coordination of various technologies to manage event operations, ticketing, security, and communication.

Success Factors:

- **Robust Project Management:** A well-structured project

management approach ensured that the IT infrastructure was delivered on time and within budget.

- **Redundancy and Security:** Comprehensive redundancy and security measures were in place to prevent disruptions and cyber threats.

- **Scalability:** The infrastructure was designed to handle an immense volume of data and traffic during the Olympics.

4. The Apple iPhone Launches:

Overview: Apple's iPhone launches have consistently set the standard for successful product launches. Each new iPhone release involves intricate IT project management, from hardware and software development to marketing and distribution.

Success Factors:

- **Innovation:** Apple's commitment to innovation and user experience drives the success of each iPhone launch.

- **Supply Chain Management:** The company's mastery of supply chain logistics ensures product availability and efficient distribution.

- **Effective Marketing:** Apple's marketing campaigns generate anticipation and excitement, contributing to record-breaking sales.

5. The Large Hadron Collider (LHC) Project:

Overview: The LHC, the world's largest and most powerful particle accelerator, is a collaborative international project aimed at advancing scientific understanding through high-energy physics experiments.

Success Factors:

- **Global Collaboration:** Scientists and engineers from around the world collaborated seamlessly on this colossal project.

- **Comprehensive Testing:** Rigorous testing and quality assurance processes were implemented to ensure the LHC's safety and functionality.

- **Robust Data Management:** Managing and analyzing the vast amounts of data generated by the LHC's experiments required cutting-edge data management solutions.

Challenges in Achieving Success:

1. **Technical Complexity:** Successful IT projects often involve cutting-edge technologies, which can be challenging to implement and maintain.

2. **Scope Changes:** Scope changes can derail even the most well-planned projects, requiring adaptability and careful management.

3. **Resource Constraints:** Budgetary limitations and resource constraints can impact project success if not managed effectively.

4. **Changing Requirements:** Evolving user requirements and technological advancements may necessitate adjustments during project execution.

5. **Risk Management:** Effective risk assessment and mitigation strategies are crucial, as unforeseen challenges can arise at any stage of a project.

In conclusion, these real-world examples of successful IT projects showcase the importance of meticulous planning, cross-functional collaboration, adaptability, and a user-centric approach. By studying these cases and applying their lessons, organizations can increase the likelihood of success in their own IT projects, whether they involve space exploration, healthcare, technology launches, infrastructure, or scientific research.

B. Project Failures and Lessons Learned: Extracting Wisdom from Setbacks

In the world of IT project management, not all ventures end in triumph. Project failures, while unfortunate, offer valuable opportunities for growth, improvement, and the acquisition of critical lessons that can inform future endeavors. In this in-depth exploration, we will delve into the realm of project failures, dissecting the common causes, repercussions, and, most importantly, the lessons learned from these setbacks.

Common Causes of Project Failures:

1. **Inadequate Planning:**

   - **Cause:** Projects initiated without a comprehensive plan often lack clear objectives, timelines, and resource allocation, leading to chaos.

   - **Lesson:** Thorough planning, including scope definition, risk assessment, and resource allocation, is essential to project success.

2. **Scope Creep:**

   - **Cause:** Expanding project scope beyond the original definition can strain resources, timelines, and budgets.

   - **Lesson:** Vigilant scope management and change control processes are crucial to prevent scope creep.

3. **Inadequate Resources:**

   - **Cause:** Projects may fail when they lack the necessary human, financial, or technological resources.

   - **Lesson:** Adequate resource planning and allocation

are essential to meet project requirements.

4. **Poor Communication:**

- **Cause:** Ineffective communication among team members, stakeholders, and management can result in misunderstandings and misalignment.

- **Lesson:** Open, transparent, and timely communication is vital for project success.

5. **Inadequate Risk Management:**

- **Cause:** Ignoring or underestimating risks can lead to project disruptions and failures.

- **Lesson:** Robust risk assessment, mitigation planning, and ongoing monitoring are critical to project resilience.

6. **Lack of Stakeholder Engagement:**

- **Cause:** Neglecting stakeholder input and expectations can lead to dissatisfaction and project failure.

- **Lesson:** Actively engage stakeholders, gather their feedback, and manage their expectations throughout the project.

7. **Technological Challenges:**

   - **Cause:** Technical issues, such as software bugs, hardware failures, or inadequate infrastructure, can disrupt projects.

   - **Lesson:** Thorough technical assessment and testing are necessary to identify and address potential issues.

8. **Misalignment with Business Goals:**

   - **Cause:** Projects that do not align with organizational objectives may be deemed unnecessary or counterproductive.

   - **Lesson:** Ensure that each project aligns with the broader strategic goals of the organization.

Repercussions of Project Failures:

1. **Financial Losses:** Project failures often result in wasted investments, budget overruns, and financial losses.

2. **Reputation Damage:** Failed projects can harm an organization's reputation, erode trust among stakeholders, and deter future investments.

3. **Resource Drain:** Unsuccessful projects consume valuable resources that could have been allocated to more promising endeavors.

4. **Employee Morale:** Project failures can demoralize team members, leading to decreased productivity and job satisfaction.

5. **Missed Opportunities:** A failed project may mean missed market opportunities or competitive advantages.

Lessons Learned from Project Failures:

1. **Thorough Planning:** Rigorous project planning, including detailed scope definition, risk assessment, and resource planning, is paramount.

2. **Effective Communication:** Open and transparent communication among team members, stakeholders, and management is critical.

3. **Stakeholder Engagement:** Actively engage stakeholders, gather their feedback, and manage their expectations throughout the project.

4. **Risk Management:** Identify, assess, and mitigate project risks proactively.

5. **Resource Allocation:** Ensure that projects are adequately resourced in terms of personnel, finances, and technology.

6. **Alignment with Strategy:** Verify that each project aligns with the organization's strategic goals.

7. **Adaptability:** Projects must be adaptable to changing conditions, requirements, and technologies.

8. **Continuous Improvement:** Implement mechanisms for ongoing evaluation and improvement, including post-project reviews.

Benefits of Embracing Failure:

Embracing and learning from project failures can lead to several benefits:

1. **Improved Decision-Making:** Lessons from past failures inform better decision-making and risk management.

2. **Innovation:** Failures can spark innovation and new approaches to problem-solving.

3. **Resilience:** Organizations become more resilient and better equipped to handle adversity.

4. **Enhanced Reputation:** Transparently acknowledging and learning from failures can enhance an organization's reputation.

5. **Organizational Learning:** A culture of learning from failures fosters continuous improvement and growth.

In conclusion, project failures, while challenging, offer valuable lessons that can ultimately contribute to an organization's success. By identifying their causes, understanding their repercussions, and extracting the wisdom they offer, organizations can build resilience, make informed decisions, and increase the likelihood of achieving their project management goals in the future.

C. Industry-specific Case Studies: Tailoring IT Project Management to Unique Challenges

In the diverse landscape of IT project management, industry-specific case studies provide invaluable insights into how project management principles are applied to address the unique challenges and opportunities within various sectors. By examining these real-world examples, organizations can gain a deeper understanding of best practices, strategies, and methodologies relevant to their industry. In this in-depth exploration, we will delve into industry-specific case studies, showcasing how IT project management is adapted to meet the distinct needs of different sectors.

1. Healthcare: Electronic Health Records (EHR) Implementation

Overview: The healthcare industry has witnessed a major transformation with the implementation of Electronic Health Records (EHR) systems. These systems enable digital storage and sharing of patient data, improving care coordination and efficiency.

Challenges:

- **Data Security:** Protecting patient data from breaches and ensuring compliance with HIPAA regulations.

- **Interoperability:** Ensuring seamless integration of EHR systems with existing infrastructure.

- **User Adoption:** Encouraging healthcare professionals to embrace and effectively use EHR systems.

Solutions:

- **Robust Data Encryption:** Implement strong encryption protocols to safeguard patient data.

- **Interoperability Standards:** Adherence to standardized data formats and interfaces for smooth integration.

- **User Training:** Comprehensive training programs to ensure healthcare professionals can use EHR systems effectively.

2. Finance: Core Banking System Upgrade

Overview: Financial institutions frequently undertake projects to upgrade their core banking systems to enhance security, customer experience, and operational efficiency.

Challenges:

- **Regulatory Compliance:** Meeting stringent financial regulations and security standards.

- **Data Migration:** Safely transferring massive volumes of customer data to the new system.

- **Business Continuity:** Ensuring uninterrupted banking services during the transition.

Solutions:

- **Regulatory Expertise:** Engaging regulatory experts to navigate complex compliance requirements.

- **Data Validation and Testing:** Rigorous testing and validation procedures to minimize data migration risks.

- **Parallel Systems:** Running both old and new systems in parallel during the transition phase.

3. Manufacturing: Enterprise Resource Planning (ERP) Implementation

Overview: Manufacturers often implement Enterprise Resource Planning (ERP) systems to streamline operations, improve supply chain management, and enhance production efficiency.

Challenges:

- **Complex Supply Chains:** Managing intricate global supply chains and vendor relationships.

- **Change Management:** Overcoming resistance to process changes among employees.

- **Integration:** Ensuring seamless integration of ERP systems with legacy manufacturing equipment.

Solutions:

- **Supply Chain Visibility:** Implementing advanced tracking and reporting tools for real-time supply chain insights.

- **Change Management Programs:** Engaging employees through training and clear communication.

- **Custom Integration Solutions:** Developing tailored interfaces for legacy equipment integration.

4. Education: Learning Management System (LMS) Implementation

Overview: Educational institutions often deploy Learning Management Systems (LMS) to facilitate online learning, manage course content, and track student progress.

Challenges:

- **User Adoption:** Encouraging educators and students to embrace the LMS.

- **Content Management:** Organizing and updating vast amounts of course content.

- **Scalability:** Ensuring the system can accommodate growing numbers of users and courses.

Solutions:

- **User Training:** Providing user-friendly interfaces and comprehensive training materials.

- **Content Management Tools:** Implementing effective content management features.

- **Scalable Infrastructure:** Designing the system architecture for scalability and performance.

5. Retail: E-commerce Platform Upgrade

Overview: Retailers continually invest in their e-commerce platforms to provide seamless online shopping experiences and stay competitive.

Challenges:

- **Cybersecurity:** Protecting customer data from online threats and breaches.

- **Mobile Optimization:** Ensuring the platform is mobile-friendly and responsive.

- **Inventory Management:** Integrating e-commerce with inventory systems for accurate stock levels.

Solutions:

- **Advanced Security Measures:** Utilizing encryption, firewalls, and continuous monitoring for cybersecurity.

- **Responsive Design:** Employing responsive web design for optimal mobile experiences.

- **Inventory Integration:** Implementing real-time inventory management systems.

Key Takeaways:

Industry-specific case studies highlight the importance of tailoring IT project management strategies to address unique challenges. These examples underscore the value of domain expertise, compliance adherence, user-centric approaches, and adaptability. By studying these cases, organizations within each industry can enhance their project management practices and improve the likelihood of successful IT projects that meet sector-specific requirements.

Conclusion

As we draw the final curtain on this journey through these pages, we invite you to reflect on the knowledge, insights, and discoveries that have unfolded before you. Our exploration of various subjects has been a captivating voyage into the depths of understanding.

In these chapters, we have ventured through the intricacies of numerous topics and examined the key concepts and findings that define these fields. It is our hope that you have found inspiration, enlightenment, and valuable takeaways that resonate with you on your own quest for knowledge.

Remember that the pursuit of understanding is an ever-evolving journey, and this book is but a milestone along the way. The world of knowledge is vast and boundless, offering endless opportunities for exploration and growth.

As you conclude this book, we encourage you to carry forward the torch of curiosity and continue your exploration of these subjects. Seek out new perspectives, engage in meaningful discussions, and embrace the thrill of lifelong learning.

We express our sincere gratitude for joining us on this intellectual adventure. Your curiosity and dedication to expanding your horizons are the driving forces behind our shared quest for wisdom and insight.

Thank you for entrusting us with a portion of your intellectual journey. May your pursuit of knowledge lead you to new heights and inspire others to embark on their own quests for understanding.

With sincere appreciation,

Nikhilesh Mishra, Author

Recap of Key Takeaways

In the journey through the multifaceted landscape of **"Mastering IT Project Management: Concepts, Techniques, and Applications"** a multitude of insights and best practices have emerged from the various topics we've explored. This recap distills the essential takeaways from each key aspect of IT project management, providing a holistic perspective on the discipline.

Introduction to IT Project Management:

- **Definition and Importance:** IT project management is the disciplined approach to planning, executing, and controlling IT projects. It is crucial for delivering projects on time, within budget, and with high quality.

- **Role of IT Project Managers:** Project managers play a central role in project success, acting as leaders, communicators, and problem solvers.

- **Key Challenges:** Common challenges include scope changes, resource constraints, and communication breakdowns.

- **The Value of Effective IT Project Management:** Effective project management improves project success rates, reduces risks, and enhances stakeholder satisfaction.

Project Initiation:

- **Project Charter and Objectives:** A well-defined project charter outlines the project's scope, objectives, stakeholders, and deliverables.

- **Stakeholder Identification and Analysis:** Identify and engage with all relevant stakeholders to manage expectations and gather requirements.

- **Feasibility Studies and Business Case Development:** Conduct feasibility studies to assess project viability and develop a compelling business case.

- **Risk Assessment and Initial Planning:** Identify and assess risks to create a risk management plan.

- **Project Scope Definition:** Clearly define and document the project scope to avoid scope creep.

Project Planning:

- **Project Schedule Development:** Create a detailed project schedule, including task dependencies and milestones.

- **Resource Allocation and Management:** Allocate resources effectively and monitor their utilization.

- **Budgeting and Cost Estimation:** Develop a realistic budget based on cost estimates and track expenses.

- **Quality Planning:** Define quality standards and processes to ensure project deliverables meet requirements.

- **Procurement and Vendor Management:** Procure necessary goods and services and manage vendor relationships.

Project Execution:

- **Team Building and Communication:** Build a cohesive project team and maintain open communication.

- **Task Execution and Tracking:** Monitor progress and track tasks to ensure they stay on schedule.

- **Change Management:** Effectively manage changes to project scope or requirements.

- **Risk Mitigation and Issue Resolution:** Continuously monitor and mitigate project risks, and address issues promptly.

- **Stakeholder Engagement and Reporting:** Keep stakeholders informed and engaged throughout the project.

Project Monitoring and Control:

- **Project Metrics and Key Performance Indicators (KPIs):** Define and track relevant metrics and KPIs to measure project performance.

- **Progress Monitoring and Reporting:** Regularly report project progress and status to stakeholders.

- **Scope Change Management:** Use formal change control processes to manage scope changes.

- **Quality Assurance and Control:** Implement quality assurance processes and conduct quality control to ensure deliverables meet standards.

- **Cost and Schedule Control:** Monitor and control project costs and schedules.

Project Risk Management:

- **Risk Identification and Assessment:** Identify, assess, and prioritize project risks.

- **Risk Response Planning:** Develop strategies to mitigate, transfer, or accept identified risks.

- **Risk Monitoring and Contingency Planning:** Continuously monitor risks and execute contingency plans when necessary.

- **Lessons Learned and Continuous Improvement:** Gather and apply lessons learned to enhance future projects.

Project Closure:

- **Project Acceptance and Deliverables Verification:** Verify that project deliverables meet acceptance criteria.

- **Transition Planning and Knowledge Transfer:** Plan for the project's transition to operational status and transfer knowledge to relevant stakeholders.

- **Project Closure Documentation:** Document project closure activities and outcomes.

- **Celebrating Successes and Post-Implementation Review:** Recognize achievements and conduct a post-implementation review to assess project outcomes.

Agile and Scrum in IT Project Management:

- **Agile Principles and Practices:** Agile emphasizes flexibility, collaboration, and iterative development.

- **Scrum Framework and Roles:** Scrum is a popular Agile framework with defined roles, ceremonies, and artifacts.

- **Implementing Agile in IT Projects:** Implement Agile practices to enhance project adaptability and customer satisfaction.

Waterfall vs. Agile: Choosing the Right Approach:

- **Waterfall Methodology:** Sequential and well-defined, suitable for projects with stable requirements.

- **Agile Methodology:** Iterative and flexible, ideal for projects with evolving or unclear requirements.

- **Hybrid Approaches:** Consider hybrid models when elements of both Waterfall and Agile are needed.

- **Selecting the Appropriate Methodology:** Choose the methodology that aligns best with project requirements and constraints.

Managing Remote and Distributed Teams:

- **Challenges of Remote Project Management:** Remote work presents unique challenges related to communication, collaboration, and team cohesion.

- **Tools and Technologies for Remote Collaboration:** Utilize technology to bridge geographical gaps and facilitate remote teamwork.

- **Best Practices for Leading Distributed Teams:** Implement best practices for managing and motivating remote team members.

IT Project Management Tools and Software:

- **Project Management Software Overview:** Explore various project management tools and software options.

- **Selection and Implementation of PM Tools:** Choose tools that align with project needs, and implement them effectively.

- **Case Studies of PM Tool Usage:** Examine real-world examples of successful tool implementations.

IT Governance and Compliance:

- **Aligning Projects with IT Governance Frameworks:** Ensure that projects align with organizational IT governance frameworks.

- **Regulatory Compliance in IT Projects:** Adhere to relevant regulations and compliance requirements.

Project Portfolio Management (PPM):

- **Principles of Project Portfolio Management:** PPM involves prioritizing and managing a portfolio of projects to maximize organizational benefits.

- **Maximizing Project Impact through PPM:** Use PPM to align projects with strategic goals and optimize resource allocation.

Project Management Office (PMO):

- **Role and Functions of a PMO:** PMOs play a crucial role in standardizing project management practices and providing support to project teams.

- **PMO's Contribution to Project Success:** PMOs contribute to project success by ensuring consistency, providing expertise, and facilitating knowledge sharing.

Change Management in IT Projects:

- **Managing Organizational Change:** Effective change management is essential to ensure smooth transitions in IT projects.

- **Stakeholder Buy-In and Communication:** Gain stakeholder buy-in through clear communication and engagement strategies.

Agile Scaling Frameworks:

- **SAFe (Scaled Agile Framework):** SAFe is a framework for scaling Agile practices to large organizations.

- **LESS (Large-Scale Scrum):** LESS is an approach that scales Scrum principles for larger teams and projects.

IT Project Management Metrics and Dashboards:

- **Measuring Project Performance:** Use metrics to assess project progress, quality, and adherence to objectives.

- **Communicating Performance with Metrics:** Effectively communicate project performance to stakeholders using metrics.

Advanced Risk Management Techniques:

- **Quantitative Risk Analysis:** Use quantitative methods to assess and prioritize project risks.

- **Monte Carlo Simulations:** Apply Monte Carlo simulations to model and analyze project uncertainties.

Cybersecurity in Project Management:

- **Integrating Cybersecurity into Projects:** Embed cybersecurity measures into project processes to protect sensitive data.

- **Protecting Sensitive Data in IT Projects:** Implement robust data protection measures to safeguard sensitive information.

Legal and Contractual Aspects:

- **Legal Considerations in IT Project Contracts:** Contracts should address legal aspects, such as obligations, liabilities, and dispute resolution.

- **Intellectual Property Rights and SLAs:** Clearly define

intellectual property rights and service-level agreements (SLAs) in contracts.

- **Dispute Resolution:** Establish mechanisms for resolving disputes in contracts.

International and Cross-Cultural Project Management:

- **Challenges of Global Project Management:** Global projects present challenges related to cultural differences, time zones, and legal regulations.

- **Best Practices in Cross-Cultural Teams:** Implement best practices to enhance collaboration and communication in diverse, cross-cultural teams.

By reflecting on these key takeaways, organizations can better navigate the complex terrain of **"Mastering IT Project Management: Concepts, Techniques, and Applications"** make informed decisions, and continuously improve their project management practices to achieve successful project outcomes.

The Future of IT Project Management

The field of IT project management is dynamic, continually evolving to adapt to technological advancements, changing business landscapes, and evolving project management methodologies. To stay ahead and ensure successful project delivery, it's crucial to anticipate and embrace emerging trends and the future of IT project management. In this comprehensive exploration, we delve into the key trends and shifts shaping the future of IT project management.

1. Agile and Beyond:

- **Agile Continues to Thrive:** Agile methodologies, such as Scrum and Kanban, will remain essential for their adaptability and customer-centric focus.

- **Scaling Agile:** Organizations will increasingly scale Agile practices to large enterprises using frameworks like SAFe (Scaled Agile Framework) and LESS (Large-Scale Scrum).

2. Hybrid Project Management:

- **Hybrid Approaches:** Many projects will adopt hybrid methodologies that blend traditional Waterfall and Agile practices, allowing for greater flexibility and risk mitigation.

3. Artificial Intelligence (AI) and Automation:

- **AI-Powered Project Management:** AI will be used to automate routine tasks, provide predictive analytics, and assist in decision-making.

- **Intelligent Project Assistants:** AI-driven project assistants will help with resource allocation, schedule optimization, and risk analysis.

4. Data-Driven Decision-Making:

- **Big Data Utilization:** Organizations will leverage big data analytics to make informed decisions, identify project trends, and predict potential issues.

- **Real-time Reporting:** Real-time project performance dashboards will become more commonplace for proactive decision-making.

5. Remote and Distributed Work:

- **Continued Remote Work:** The trend of remote work and virtual teams will persist, requiring enhanced tools and methodologies for remote project management.

- **Global Collaboration:** Collaborating with international teams will be the norm, necessitating effective cross-cultural communication and collaboration strategies.

6. Sustainability and Green IT:

- **Environmental Concerns:** Green IT initiatives will gain prominence as organizations strive to reduce their carbon footprint, influencing project management decisions.

- **Sustainable Project Practices:** IT project managers will consider sustainability in project planning, procurement, and resource management.

7. Cybersecurity Integration:

- **Cybersecurity by Design:** Cybersecurity measures will be integrated into project management processes from the outset, with a focus on protecting sensitive data.

8. DevOps and Continuous Delivery:

- **DevOps Integration:** IT projects will increasingly adopt DevOps practices to streamline software development, testing, and deployment.

- **Continuous Delivery:** Continuous integration and continuous delivery (CI/CD) pipelines will become standard for software projects.

9. Project Management Software Evolution:

- **AI-Enhanced Tools:** Project management software will incorporate AI for better resource allocation, risk assessment, and automated reporting.

- **Enhanced Collaboration:** Tools will offer improved collaboration features for remote and distributed teams.

10. Soft Skills and Leadership:

- **Emphasis on Soft Skills:** IT project managers will need strong soft skills such as communication, adaptability, and emotional intelligence to lead diverse teams effectively.

11. Sustainable Practices:

- **Green Project Management:** Sustainable project management practices will become essential, focusing on reducing waste, energy consumption, and environmental impact.

12. Agile Portfolio Management:

- **Portfolio Agility:** Organizations will extend Agile principles to portfolio management, allowing for more responsive allocation of resources to strategic initiatives.

13. Outcome-Based Metrics:

- **Focus on Outcomes:** Metrics will shift from measuring outputs to outcomes, emphasizing the value delivered to stakeholders and the achievement of strategic objectives.

14. Ethical Considerations:

- **Ethical Project Management:** Ethical considerations, such as data privacy and responsible AI use, will become integral to project planning and execution.

15. Continuous Learning:

- **Lifelong Learning:** IT project managers will need to embrace continuous learning to stay updated on evolving technologies and methodologies.

16. Resilience Planning:

- **Resilience in Projects:** Project managers will incorporate resilience planning to address unforeseen disruptions, whether they be pandemics, natural disasters, or cyberattacks.

17. Sustainability and Social Responsibility:

- **Social Responsibility:** Organizations will increasingly prioritize projects that align with social and environmental goals, reflecting a broader shift toward sustainability.

18. Blockchain Integration:

- **Blockchain in Project Management:** Blockchain technology will be employed for enhanced transparency, traceability, and security in project documentation and transactions.

19. Quantum Computing:

- **Quantum Impact:** As quantum computing matures, it will have applications in complex simulations, optimization, and cryptography, impacting project management in certain domains.

20. Ecosystem Thinking:

- **Ecosystem Collaboration:** IT project managers will consider the broader ecosystem of stakeholders, partners, and competitors when planning and executing projects.

In conclusion, the future of IT project management is marked by adaptability, technology-driven transformation, and a heightened emphasis on sustainability, ethics, and collaboration. Successful IT project managers will need to embrace these trends, continuously upgrade their skills, and adopt innovative approaches to navigate the evolving landscape effectively. Staying agile, data-driven, and ethically responsible will be essential in shaping the future of IT project management.

Glossary of Terms

In the realm of IT project management, a robust understanding of terminology is crucial for effective communication, collaboration, and project success. This glossary provides an in-depth reference to key IT project management terms, ensuring clarity and alignment among project stakeholders.

1. Agile:

- **Definition:** An iterative and flexible project management approach that emphasizes customer collaboration, adaptability to change, and delivering value incrementally.

- **Usage:** Agile methodologies, such as Scrum and Kanban, are commonly used in IT projects for rapid development and customer responsiveness.

2. Backlog:

- **Definition:** A prioritized list of tasks, features, or user stories that need to be completed in an Agile project. It represents the work to be done.

- **Usage:** The product backlog in Scrum is continually refined and reprioritized during sprint planning.

3. Change Control:

- **Definition:** A process for documenting, evaluating, and approving or rejecting changes to the project scope, schedule, or resources.

- **Usage:** Change control ensures that changes are managed systematically to prevent scope creep.

4. Critical Path:

- **Definition:** The sequence of tasks in a project that, if delayed, would cause the project's overall duration to extend. It represents the longest path through the project schedule.

- **Usage:** Identifying the critical path helps project managers focus on tasks that are most critical to project completion.

5. Deliverable:

- **Definition:** A tangible or intangible output of a project, such as a report, software module, or completed phase, that must be produced to meet project objectives.

- **Usage:** Deliverables are often specified in the project scope and must be approved by stakeholders.

6. Earned Value Management (EVM):

- **Definition:** A project performance measurement technique that assesses a project's progress and performance based on planned versus actual work completed and cost incurred.

- **Usage:** EVM helps project managers evaluate project cost and schedule performance.

7. Gantt Chart:

- **Definition:** A visual representation of a project schedule that displays tasks, milestones, and their durations on a timeline.

- **Usage:** Gantt charts provide a clear overview of project tasks and their dependencies.

8. Kanban:

- **Definition:** A visual project management method that uses boards and cards to visualize work in progress, allowing teams to optimize workflow and manage tasks.

- **Usage:** Kanban boards are used to track the status of tasks in a visual and transparent manner.

9. Milestone:

- **Definition:** A significant event or achievement in a project, often used to mark the completion of a phase or a critical task.

- **Usage:** Milestones help project teams track progress and ensure that key project objectives are met.

10. Project Charter:

- **Definition:** A formal document that authorizes the initiation of a project, outlining its objectives, scope, stakeholders, and high-level risks and assumptions.

- **Usage:** The project charter provides a clear project mandate and aligns stakeholders' expectations.

11. Risk Register:

- **Definition:** A document that identifies, assesses, and tracks project risks, including their likelihood, impact, and mitigation strategies.

- **Usage:** The risk register helps project managers proactively manage and mitigate potential threats.

12. Scope Creep:

- **Definition:** The uncontrolled expansion of a project's scope, typically involving the addition of features or tasks without proper authorization.

- **Usage:** Scope creep can lead to project delays and budget overruns.

13. Stakeholder:

- **Definition:** Any individual, group, or organization that has an interest in or is affected by the project's outcomes.

- **Usage:** Effective stakeholder management is essential for project success and involves communication and engagement strategies.

14. Sprint:

- **Definition:** In Scrum, a time-boxed iteration of work, usually lasting two to four weeks, during which a set of user stories is completed.

- **Usage:** Sprints facilitate the incremental delivery of functionality in Agile projects.

15. Waterfall Methodology:

- **Definition:** A traditional project management approach characterized by sequential phases (requirements, design, implementation, testing, deployment) with minimal iteration.

- **Usage:** Waterfall is often used for projects with well-defined requirements.

16. Work Breakdown Structure (WBS):

- **Definition:** A hierarchical decomposition of the project scope into smaller, manageable work packages, tasks, and subtasks.

- **Usage:** WBS provides a structured approach to project

planning and task assignment.

17. Quality Assurance (QA):

- **Definition:** The systematic process of ensuring that project deliverables meet defined quality standards and that project processes are effective.

- **Usage:** QA activities aim to prevent defects and ensure project success.

18. Risk Mitigation:

- **Definition:** The process of taking proactive actions to reduce the likelihood or impact of identified risks on a project.

- **Usage:** Risk mitigation strategies are implemented to minimize potential negative project outcomes.

19. Scrum Master:

- **Definition:** In Scrum, a role responsible for facilitating and coaching the Scrum team, removing impediments, and ensuring adherence to Scrum practices.

- **Usage:** The Scrum Master plays a crucial role in enabling the team's productivity and effectiveness.

20. User Acceptance Testing (UAT):

- **Definition:** The phase of testing in which end-users evaluate and validate the functionality and usability of a software product before its final release.

- **Usage:** UAT ensures that the product aligns with user expectations.

This glossary serves as a valuable reference for both seasoned IT project managers and those new to the field, fostering effective communication and promoting a common understanding of essential project management concepts and terminology.

Resources and References

As you reach the final pages of this book by Nikhilesh Mishra, consider it not an ending but a stepping stone. The pursuit of knowledge is an unending journey, and the world of information is boundless.

Discover a World Beyond These Pages

We extend a warm invitation to explore a realm of boundless learning and discovery through our dedicated online platform: **www.nikhileshmishra.com**. Here, you will unearth a carefully curated trove of resources and references to empower your quest for wisdom.

Unleash the Potential of Your Mind

- **Digital Libraries:** Immerse yourself in vast digital libraries, granting access to books, research papers, and academic treasures.

- **Interactive Courses:** Engage with interactive courses and lectures from world-renowned institutions, nurturing your thirst for knowledge.

- **Enlightening Talks:** Be captivated by enlightening talks delivered by visionaries and experts from diverse fields.

- **Community Connections:** Connect with a global community of like-minded seekers, engage in meaningful discussions, and share your knowledge journey.

Your Journey Has Just Begun

Your journey as a seeker of knowledge need not end here. Our website awaits your exploration, offering a gateway to an infinite universe of insights and references tailored to ignite your intellectual curiosity.

Acknowledgments

As I stand at this pivotal juncture, reflecting upon the completion of this monumental work, I am overwhelmed with profound gratitude for the exceptional individuals who have been instrumental in shaping this remarkable journey.

In Loving Memory

To my father, **Late Shri Krishna Gopal Mishra,** whose legacy of wisdom and strength continues to illuminate my path, even in his physical absence, I offer my deepest respect and heartfelt appreciation.

The Pillars of Support

My mother, **Mrs. Vijay Kanti Mishra,** embodies unwavering resilience and grace. Your steadfast support and unwavering faith in my pursuits have been the bedrock of my journey.

To my beloved wife, **Mrs. Anshika Mishra,** your unshakable belief in my abilities has been an eternal wellspring of motivation. Your constant encouragement has propelled me to reach new heights.

My daughter, **Miss Aarvi Mishra,** infuses my life with boundless joy and unbridled inspiration. Your insatiable curiosity serves as a constant reminder of the limitless power of exploration and discovery.

Brothers in Arms

To my younger brothers, **Mr. Ashutosh Mishra** and **Mr. Devashish Mishra,** who have steadfastly stood by my side, offering unwavering support and shared experiences that underscore the strength of familial bonds.

A Journey Shared

This book is a testament to the countless hours of dedication and effort that have gone into its creation. I am immensely grateful for the privilege of sharing my knowledge and insights with a global audience.

Readers, My Companions

To all the readers who embark on this intellectual journey alongside me, your curiosity and unquenchable thirst for knowledge inspire me to continually push the boundaries of understanding in the realm of cloud computing.

With profound appreciation and sincere gratitude,

Nikhilesh Mishra

September 08, 2023

About the Author

Nikhilesh Mishra is an extraordinary visionary, propelled by an insatiable curiosity and an unyielding passion for innovation. With a relentless commitment to exploring the boundaries of knowledge and technology, Nikhilesh has embarked on an exceptional journey to unravel the intricate complexities of our world.

Hailing from the vibrant and diverse landscape of India, Nikhilesh's pursuit of knowledge has driven him to plunge deep into the world of discovery and understanding from a remarkably young age. His unwavering determination and quest for innovation have not only cemented his position as a thought leader but have also earned him global recognition in the ever-evolving realm of technology and human understanding.

Over the years, Nikhilesh has not only mastered the art of translating complex concepts into accessible insights but has also crafted a unique talent for inspiring others to explore the limitless possibilities of human potential.

Nikhilesh's journey transcends the mere boundaries of expertise; it is a transformative odyssey that challenges conventional wisdom and redefines the essence of exploration. His commitment to pushing the boundaries and reimagining the norm serves as a luminous beacon of inspiration to all those who aspire to make a profound impact in the world of knowledge.

As you navigate the intricate corridors of human understanding and innovation, you will not only gain insight into Nikhilesh's expertise but also experience his unwavering dedication to empowering readers like you. Prepare to be enthralled as he seamlessly melds intricate insights with real-world applications, igniting the flames of curiosity and innovation within each reader.

Nikhilesh Mishra's work extends beyond the realm of authorship; it is a reflection of his steadfast commitment to shaping the future of knowledge and exploration. It is an embodiment of his boundless dedication to disseminating wisdom for the betterment of individuals worldwide.

Prepare to be inspired, enlightened, and empowered as you embark on this transformative journey alongside Nikhilesh Mishra. Your understanding of the world will be forever enriched, and your passion for exploration and innovation will reach new heights under his expert guidance.

Sincerely, **A Fellow Explorer**

Notes

Notes

Notes

Notes

Notes

Notes

www.ingramcontent.com/pod-product-compliance
Lightning Source LLC
LaVergne TN
LVHW051421050326
832903LV00030BC/2926